Astrology Workbook 3-in-1

Unlock Your Birth Chart, Discover Your Cosmic Identity, and Use the Zodiac to Navigate Life with Purpose

Your Free Gift
(only available for a limited time)

Thanks for getting this book! If you want to learn more about various spirituality topics, then join Mari Silva's community and get a free guided meditation MP3 for awakening your third eye. This guided meditation mp3 is designed to open and strengthen ones third eye so you can experience a higher state of consciousness. Simply visit the link below the image to get started.

https://spiritualityspot.com/meditation

Or, Scan the QR code!

Table of Contents

Overall Introduction: The Science and Symbolism of the Stars

Human beings have looked to the sky to explain life on Earth for over five thousand years. This practice is not merely a modern hobby. It is one of the oldest forms of data collection in human history. Long before the invention of the telescope, ancient civilizations in Mesopotamia recorded the movements of the planets with mathematical precision. These early observers noticed that certain celestial cycles aligned with the flooding of rivers, the success of harvests, and the shifts in social leadership.

To understand astrology today, we must look at its history as a bridge between astronomy and social science. In ancient Babylon, the sky was a massive clock. By 700 BCE, scholars had produced the *MUL.APIN*, a collection of clay tablets that cataloged the rising and setting of stars. These records were the first attempts to turn the chaos of the night sky into a predictable system. They treated the planets as variables in a large-scale experiment. When a specific planet returned to a certain point in the sky, they looked for patterns in human behavior that matched its previous visit.

This workbook treats the birth chart with that same objective lens. While many view the zodiac as a source of fortune-telling, this book approaches it as a tool for archetypal analysis. An archetype is a universal pattern or image that exists in the collective human mind. This concept was popularized by the psychiatrist Carl Jung in the early 20th century. Jung noted that the symbols found in astrology, such as the warrior, the nurturer, and the communicator, mirror the fundamental parts of the human psyche. He often used birth charts in his clinical work to help patients see their internal contradictions more clearly.

Recent research in chronobiology also offers a modern perspective on how our birth timing might affect us. Studies, such as those published in *Nature Neuroscience*, suggest that the season of a person's birth can influence their circadian rhythms and personality traits. For instance, individuals born in winter months may show different levels of dopamine and serotonin compared to those born in summer. While this is not a direct proof of planetary influence, it shows that the environment at the moment of birth has a measurable impact on biological development.

This book is divided into three books to help you apply these concepts practically.

- **Book 1** focuses on the mechanics of your birth chart. You will learn how to read the twelve houses and the placements of the planets.

- **Book 2** moves into your identity. We look at the elements and the deeper symbols that define your temperament.

- **Book 3** teaches you how to use these cycles to make better decisions in your career and relationships.

Each chapter ends with a mini-workbook section. These are not just for reading; they are for doing. You will need your birth chart ready as you progress. If you do not have one, several reputable resources in the back of this book can help you generate one using your birth date, time, and location.

Mini-Workbook: Setting Your Objective

Before you begin with the first book, take a moment to record your current baseline. This helps you track how your perspective changes as you work through the chapters.

1. **Current Knowledge:** On a scale of 1 to 10, how well do you understand the symbols in your birth chart right now?

2. **The Primary Goal:** What is one specific area of your life, such as communication, career, or emotional habits, where you want more clarity?

3. **The Data Check:** Do you have your exact birth time from a birth certificate? (Accuracy is vital for the "House" system discussed in Book 1).

BOOK ONE
Unlock Your Birth Chart

Introduction:
Why the Exact Moment of Birth Serves as a Personal Map

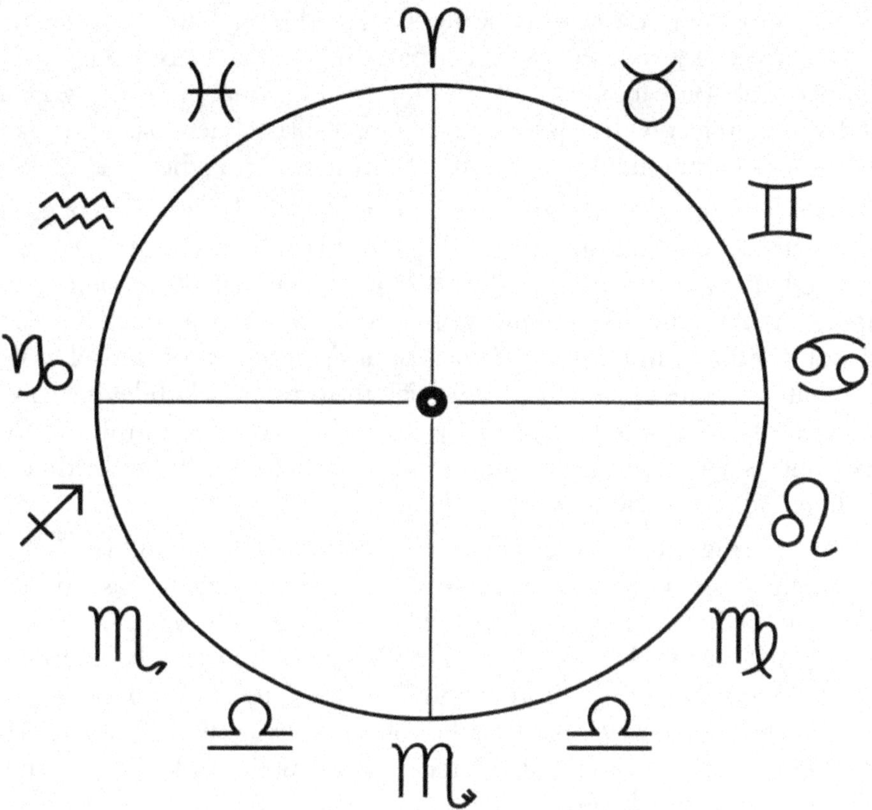

When you were born, the world did not just receive a new life; it captured a specific arrangement of the cosmos. Every person carries an invisible map, drawn at the precise second they enter the world. This map is not made of paper and ink but of planetary positions and celestial degrees. It is called a birth chart, or a natal chart. It captures the unique cosmic signature of your beginnings.

To understand this concept, it helps to think of the solar system as a dynamic, constantly moving clock. At the moment of your first breath, all the planets, the Sun, and the Moon were in specific places against the backdrop of the zodiac signs. These positions are then marked onto a circular diagram, creating a snapshot of the sky from your specific vantage point on Earth.

The Historical Evolution of the Celestial Map

The idea of the birth chart as a personal blueprint is far from a modern invention. It dates back to the sophisticated observations of ancient Egypt and Mesopotamia. Early astronomers were the first to notice that the patterns in the sky seemed to reflect patterns on Earth. By roughly 2,400 years ago, the Babylonians had developed the concept of the zodiac, a 360-degree circle divided into twelve equal parts. Each part was named after a constellation that the Sun passed through during the year.

While we often think of these ancient people as primitive, their mathematical rigor was staggering. They didn't just look at the stars; they calculated their movements with such precision that they could predict eclipses and planetary conjunctions years in advance. The Greek philosopher Plato, in his work *Timaeus,* discussed the concept of a "world soul" that was interwoven with celestial movements. While he was not looking at "horoscopes" in the way we see them on a smartphone today, his writings suggested a profound connection between the individual soul and the structure of the universe.

Later, during the Hellenistic period, around the 1st century BCE, the mathematical techniques became sophisticated enough to cast individual birth charts. This was a massive shift in human thought. Before this, astrology was primarily used to predict the fate of kings or the success of a harvest. With the rise of "horoscopic astrology" in Alexandria, the focus moved from national events to the life of the individual. This was the birth of the idea that a person's character and life path could be understood through the lens of the stars.

The Chart as a Map of Potential

It is a common mistake to think of a birth chart as a fixed destiny or a "fortune" that cannot be changed. Instead, it is a diagram of potential. Think of it as a musical score written for an orchestra. The notes are all on the page, but the way they are played depends on the musicians, the conductor, and the environment of the concert hall. The tempo, the dynamics, and the emotional weight of the performance can vary wildly even if the notes remain the same.

Similarly, your birth chart shows the themes and energies present in your life. It outlines your natural talents, your emotional responses, and the types of challenges you might face. How you engage with these themes is entirely up to you. For example, a chart might show a strong influence of Mars, the planet associated with action, drive, and heat. In a person's life, this might manifest as a natural gift for leadership and physical stamina. However, if left unchecked or unexamined, that same energy might manifest as a tendency toward conflict or impulsivity. The chart shows the "energy" of Mars; it does not dictate whether you use it to build or to burn.

This distinction is vital for the modern reader. We are not looking for "predictions" in these pages. We are looking for a vocabulary. Most of us struggle to describe why we react to stress the way we do, or why certain types of careers feel draining while others feel like home. The birth chart gives us a framework to identify these internal drives. It moves the conversation from "Why am I like this?" to "This is an active theme in my life; how can I work with it?"

Archetypes and the Human Psyche

Modern psychology offers fascinating parallels to this ancient practice. The Swiss psychiatrist Carl Jung is perhaps the most famous figure to bridge these two worlds. Jung believed that the symbols found in astrology, the Warrior, the Mother, the Trickster, and the Sage, were part of the "collective unconscious." These are archetypes, or universal patterns of behavior and imagery that exist in all humans regardless of their culture or upbringing.

Jung often used birth charts in his clinical practice. He found that they were incredibly useful for helping patients see their internal contradictions. For instance, a patient might feel torn between a desire for security (represented by the Moon in a sign like Taurus) and a deep need for total independence and change (represented by Uranus). By seeing these two forces as distinct "players" in their chart, the patient could stop feeling like they were "broken" and start seeing themselves as a complex system of competing needs.

Recent research in the field of chronobiology, the study of biological rhythms, adds another layer to this. A study published in *Nature Neuroscience* in 2010 found that the light cycles experienced by an infant at birth can "imprint" their biological clock. This imprinting affects how the brain regulates mood and responses to stress throughout life.

While this doesn't prove that "Jupiter" is making you lucky, it does suggest that the environment at the exact moment of your birth has a measurable, lasting impact on your neurological development. Astrology was, in many ways, the first attempt to map these environmental impacts.

The Three Pillars: Time, Date, and Place

To build an accurate map of your identity, we need three pieces of data. Each one is essential for a different reason:

1. **Your Birth Date:** This is the most basic piece of the puzzle. It tells us where the Sun was in the zodiac. The Sun moves about one degree per day, so your date identifies your "Sun Sign." In the 1930s, newspapers began printing "Sun Sign" horoscopes, which led most people to believe that this single sign is the entirety of astrology. In reality, the Sun is only one piece of a much larger puzzle.

2. **Your Birth Location:** The Earth is a sphere, and at any given moment, the sky looks different depending on where you are standing. If you were born in London at the same time someone was born in Tokyo, your charts would be different. The planets would be in different "Houses" because your perspective of the horizon changed. Longitude and latitude are the coordinates that lock your chart to the Earth.

3. **Your Birth Time:** This is the most critical variable. The Earth rotates on its axis every 24 hours. This means that the zodiac signs on the horizon change about every two hours. The sign that was rising in the East at the moment you were born is called your **Ascendant** or **Rising Sign**. This sign determines the layout of your entire chart. It sets the "Houses," which are the twelve areas of life (money, family, health, etc.). If your birth time is off by even thirty minutes, the entire structure of your map can shift.

Reading the Wheel: Signs and Houses

When you look at your chart, you see a wheel divided into twelve sections. Think of this wheel as a stage.

- **The Planets** are the actors. They represent *what* is happening (e.g., Mercury represents communication, Venus represents values).

- **The Zodiac Signs** are the costumes. They represent *how* the actors behave (e.g., Mercury in Aries communicates quickly and boldly; Mercury in Pisces communicates through intuition and metaphors).

- **The Houses** are the sets or locations. They represent *where* the action takes place (e.g., Mercury in the 10th House of career means your communication skills are focused on your public life).

Understanding this triad is the key to moving past the surface level of astrology. Many people read that they are a "Leo" and feel it doesn't fit them because they are shy. However, a look at their full chart might reveal that while their Sun is in Leo, their Mercury (communication) and Ascendant (the mask they show the world) are in more reserved, analytical signs like Virgo or Scorpio. The chart accounts for the complexity and the contradictions that make us human.

The Practical Utility of the Map

Why do this work? The reviews of many beginner astrology books often mention that the content feels "too airy" or "not practical enough." Our goal here is the opposite. We use this map to navigate the very real, often difficult parts of life.

By identifying the "stress points" in your chart, areas where planets are in challenging angles to one another, you can anticipate recurring patterns. If you notice that you consistently have trouble with authority figures, you might find a specific configuration in your 10th House or involving the planet Saturn. Knowing this doesn't "fix" the problem instantly, but it changes your relationship to it. Instead of feeling like a victim of circumstance, you can observe the pattern as it happens and choose a different response.

This workbook is designed to be a companion. As we move through the chapters on the "Big Three" (Sun, Moon, and Ascendant), the personal planets, and the outer planets, you will be building your own interpretation bit by bit. We are not just giving you information; we are training you to be an analyst of your own life.

Synthesizing the Data

As you begin to fill in your workbook, remember that no single placement defines you. A birth chart is a synthesis. Just as you cannot understand a person by looking only at their hand or their eye, you cannot understand a chart by looking only at one planet. You must look at how the different parts speak to one another.

Are your planets mostly clustered in the bottom half of the circle? This might suggest a more private, introspective life focus. Are they mostly in the top half? This often points to a life lived very much in the public eye or through career achievements. This "geometry" of the chart provides a bird's-eye view of your life's orientation before we even get into the specifics of the signs.

The journey we are starting is one of radical self-honesty. Using the zodiac as a map requires you to look at your strengths with pride and your shadows with curiosity. It asks you to consider that there is a rhyme and a reason to the way you interact with the world.

Mini-Workbook: Your Foundational Data

This section begins your active engagement with your birth chart. Please take a moment to gather the necessary information to generate your chart. If you have already done so, you can fill in the initial data:

1. **Full Name:** ____

2. **Date of Birth:** ____

3. **Exact Time of Birth:** ____

   (Check your birth certificate. Hospital records are more reliable than parental memory.)

4. **Birth City and Country:** ______________________________________

5. **Identify Your Hemispheres:** Look at your chart. Are more planets located in the top half (Above the Horizon) or the bottom half (Below the Horizon)?

   - **Top Heavy:** Focus on public life, career, and social status.
   - **Bottom Heavy:** Focus on private life, family, and internal growth.

6. **The Immediate Reaction:** Looking at the "web" of lines in the center of your chart wheel, does it look crowded or sparse? What is your first emotional reaction to seeing your life "mapped" out this way?

Chapter 1: The Foundation of the Houses

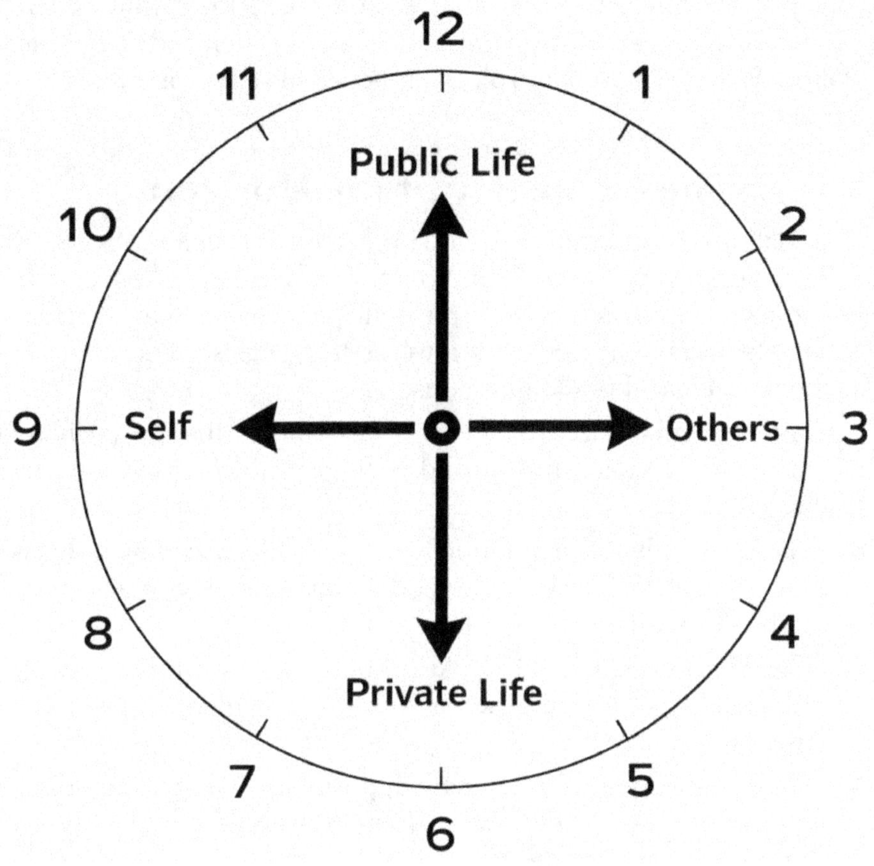

Spatial Orientation and the Twelve Sectors of Life

If the planets are the actors in your life story and the signs are the roles they play, then the houses are the stages where the action occurs. Without the houses, astrology would remain a floating, abstract map of the sky. The house system is what grounds the celestial movements into the local, physical reality of your life on Earth. While the zodiac signs tell us about your temperament and character, the houses tell us about your circumstances.

They reveal where your energy is most likely to be spent, whether in the quiet privacy of the home, the busy halls of a career, or the complex dynamics of a partnership.

The houses are 12 distinct sectors of the sky, but they are defined by your specific location at the moment of your birth. This is why the house system is often referred to as "local space." While everyone born on a specific day will have the Sun in the same sign, their houses will be completely different based on the time and city of their birth. This spatial orientation is what makes astrology a personalized tool rather than a general one.

The Geometry of the Horizon

The foundation of the house system is the Earth's rotation. As the Earth spins on its axis every twenty-four hours, the entire circle of the zodiac appears to rise, culminate, and set from our perspective. This creates four critical points in any birth chart, known as the "angles." These angles are the mathematical backbone of the houses.

1. **The Ascendant (AC):** This is the point in the East where the zodiac was rising at the second of your birth. It marks the start of the 1st House.

2. **The Descendant (DC):** Directly opposite the Ascendant, this is the point in the West where the zodiac was setting. It marks the start of the 7th House.

3. **The Medium Coeli (MC):** Also known as the Midheaven, this is the highest point in the sky at your birth. It marks the start of the 10th House.

4. **The Imum Coeli (IC):** Directly opposite the Midheaven, this is the lowest point in the sky, often associated with the midnight position. It marks the start of the 4th House.

These four points divide the chart into four quadrants. Each quadrant is then further divided into three sections, creating the twelve houses. This division is not just symbolic; it follows the path of the Sun's daily movement. The houses represent the literal orientation of the planets relative to the horizon at the time you were born.

Historical Origins:
From Octotopos to the Twelve Houses

The concept of dividing the sky into sectors did not begin with twelve houses. In the earliest forms of Hellenistic astrology, practitioners often used a system of eight sectors, known as the *Octotopos*. Each of these eight sections was associated with a specific life theme, such as health, wealth, or travel. However, as mathematical techniques improved and the desire for more nuanced detail grew, the system evolved into the twelve-house structure we use today.

By the 1st and 2nd centuries CE, astronomers like Claudius Ptolemy were refining the definitions of these sectors. In his seminal work, *Tetrabiblos*, Ptolemy laid the groundwork for how we perceive the "strength" of a planet based on its house position. He noted that planets near the angles (the 1st, 4th, 7th, and 10th houses) were much more active and visible in a person's life than planets tucked away in the "cadent" or falling houses. This was the beginning of "house significations"—the specific list of life topics assigned to each sector.

A Detailed Tour of the Twelve Houses

To use this workbook effectively, you must understand the specific "territory" each house governs. Each house follows a logical progression, starting from the self and moving outward into the collective world.

House 1: The House of Self and Appearance

This is the most personal part of the chart. Because it contains the Ascendant, it represents your physical body, your vitality, and the "mask" you wear when meeting others. It is the filter through which you view the world and how the world views you. If you have planets here, they color your entire personality and physical presence.

House 2: Values and Personal Resources

Moving from the "who" to the "what," the 2nd House governs what you own and what you value. This includes your finances, your possessions, and your sense of self-worth. In a practical sense, it shows your attitude toward money and your ability to sustain yourself.

House 3: Communication and Immediate Environment

The 3rd House is about local movement and information. it governs your siblings, your neighbors, primary education, and how you process data. It is the house of the "concrete mind." If you have a busy 3rd House, your life is likely filled with short trips, constant emails, and a deep need to stay curious.

House 4: Home, Roots, and Ancestry

At the very bottom of the chart, the 4th House represents your foundations. This is your private life, your home environment, and your connection to your parents or ancestors. It is the "soil" from which you grow. It shows where you go to feel safe and where you withdraw from the public eye.

House 5: Creativity, Pleasure, and Children

This is the house of "self-expression." It governs everything you do for fun, including hobbies, romance, artistic projects, and children. It is about the joy of being alive and the things you "create" and put out into the world for the sake of play.

House 6: Work, Health, and Daily Routines

The 6th House is often overlooked, but it is the house of "maintenance." It governs your daily job (not your career, but the tasks you do every day), your physical health, and your habits. It is the house of service and the small, repetitive actions that keep life running smoothly.

House 7: Partnerships and Open Enemies

Directly across from the 1st House of Self is the 7th House of "The Other." This governs all one-on-one committed relationships, including marriage and business partnerships. Interestingly, it also governs "open enemies": people with whom you have a clear, direct conflict. It shows what you look for in others to balance yourself.

House 8: Shared Resources and Transformation

The 8th House is one of the most complex sectors. It deals with things you share with others: joint finances, inheritances, and intimacy. On a deeper level, it governs the cycles of birth, death, and psychological transformation. It is where we face the things we cannot control.

House 9: Higher Learning and Long-Distance Travel

Opposite the 3rd House of local knowledge is the 9th House of "expanded horizons." This governs university education, philosophy, religion, and foreign travel. It is where we seek meaning and try to understand the "big picture" of life.

House 10: Career and Public Reputation

Located at the highest point of the chart (the Midheaven), the 10th House is your "calling." It represents your career, your status in society, and your public achievements. While the 6th House is about your daily work, the 10th House is about your legacy and what you are known for by the world.

House 11: Community, Hopes, and Friendships

The 11th House is the sector of "the collective." It governs your friendships, your social circles, and your involvement in groups or organizations. It also represents your long-term goals and the "hopes and wishes" you have for the future of society.

House 12: The Hidden Realm and Solitude

The final house is the most mysterious. It governs the things that are hidden from view: the subconscious, secrets, hospitals, and places of retreat. It is the "closet" of the chart where we store things we aren't ready to face. Planets here often operate in a way that is invisible to the individual but clear to others.

The Three Categories of Houses

To deepen your understanding, we categorize these houses into three groups based on their "strength" and how they initiate energy. This is a technical distinction used by professional astrologers to see which areas of life will be the most active for you.

- **Angular Houses (1, 4, 7, 10):** These are the most powerful houses. Planets here are "loud" and take direct action. If you have many planets in angular houses, your life is likely characterized by significant outward events and clear beginnings.

- **Succedent Houses (2, 5, 8, 11):** These houses follow the angles. Their job is to stabilize and consolidate the energy initiated by the angles. They represent resources and steady growth.

- **Cadent Houses (3, 6, 9, 12):** These are the "falling" houses. They are the least stable and often represent transition, learning, and the distribution of energy. Planets here are more internal and less likely to result in major "public" events.

Psychological Houses: The Internal Stage

In modern archetypal psychology, the houses are viewed as a map of psychological development. The 1st through 6th houses represent the "Development of the Self." They focus on your body, your money, your mind, your home, and your habits. The 7th through 12th houses represent the "Development of the Self in Relation to the World." They focus on your partners, your transformations, your beliefs, your career, and your social impact.

This division mirrors the human maturation process. We start by focusing on our immediate needs and slowly expand our consciousness to include the needs of others and the requirements of society. When you look at your birth chart, see which "hemisphere" is more populated. A chart with most planets in the bottom half suggests an individual whose primary focus is internal and personal. A chart with planets in the top half suggests someone whose life is deeply intertwined with social structures and public roles.

The Empty House Myth

One of the most common questions from beginners is: "What if a house is empty?" It is mathematically impossible to have a planet in every house. Most people will have several "empty" houses. This does not mean that area of your life is "missing" or "unimportant." It simply means there isn't a specific "actor" stationed there permanently.

To understand an empty house, you look at the sign on the "cusp" (the beginning line) of that house. The planet that "rules" that sign becomes the landlord of the empty house. For example, if your 2nd House of money is empty but starts in the sign of Taurus, you look to where Venus (the ruler of Taurus) is located in your chart. Venus will tell the story of your finances. This adds a layer of connectivity to the chart, showing how different areas of life are linked through planetary ownership.

Applying the House System to Real Life

Authoritative astrology relies on the "Five-Degree Rule." If a planet is within five degrees of the next house's cusp, it is often interpreted as being active in *both* houses, with a stronger pull toward the upcoming house. This is because the cusp is a point of high energy. Think of it like standing in a doorway; you are technically in one room, but you can see and hear everything in the next one.

When you begin to analyze your own chart, start with the angles. Look at your 1st, 4th, 7th, and 10th houses. These are the pillars of your life. Any planet sitting on these angles will be a dominant force in your personality and life story. For example, Saturn on the Midheaven (10th House) often indicates a person who takes their career extremely seriously and may face heavy responsibilities early in life. Conversely, Jupiter on the Ascendant (1st House) often shows a person with an optimistic, expansive presence.

Mini-Workbook: Mapping Your Houses

Now it is time to look at the "Stage" of your own life. Use the birth chart you generated in the Introduction to fill out this section:

1. **Identify Your Angles:** Record the zodiac sign and the exact degree for each of your four main angles:

    -   **Ascendant (1st House Cusp):** _______________________________
        -   o Sign: ____
        -   o Degree: ____
    -   **IC (4th House Cusp):** ___________________________________
        -   o Sign: ____
        -   o Degree: ____
    -   **Descendant (7th House Cusp):** ___________________________
        -   o Sign: ____
        -   o Degree: ____
    -   **Midheaven (10th House Cusp):** ___________________________
        -   o Sign: ____
        -   o Degree: ____

2. **The House Population Count:** Count how many planets (include the Sun and Moon) are in each quadrant:
    -   o Lower-Left (Houses 1-3 - Private Self): _______________
    -   o Lower-Right (Houses 4-6 - Private Others): ___________
    -   o Upper-Right (Houses 7-9 - Public Others): ___________
    -   o Upper-Left (Houses 10-12 - Public Self): _______________

3. **The "Busy" House:** Which house in your chart has the most planets?

____

____

____

   o   Looking at the list of house meanings above, does this area of life (e.g., career, home, communication) feel like a major focus for you? Why?

4. **The Empty House Check:** Choose one house that is empty in your chart. ____

   o   Which sign is on the cusp of that house? ______________

   o   Search for the "ruler" of that sign (e.g., Mars rules Aries, Venus rules Taurus). In which house is that ruling planet located? ____

   o   *This shows the link between the two areas of life.*

Chapter 2: The Big Three

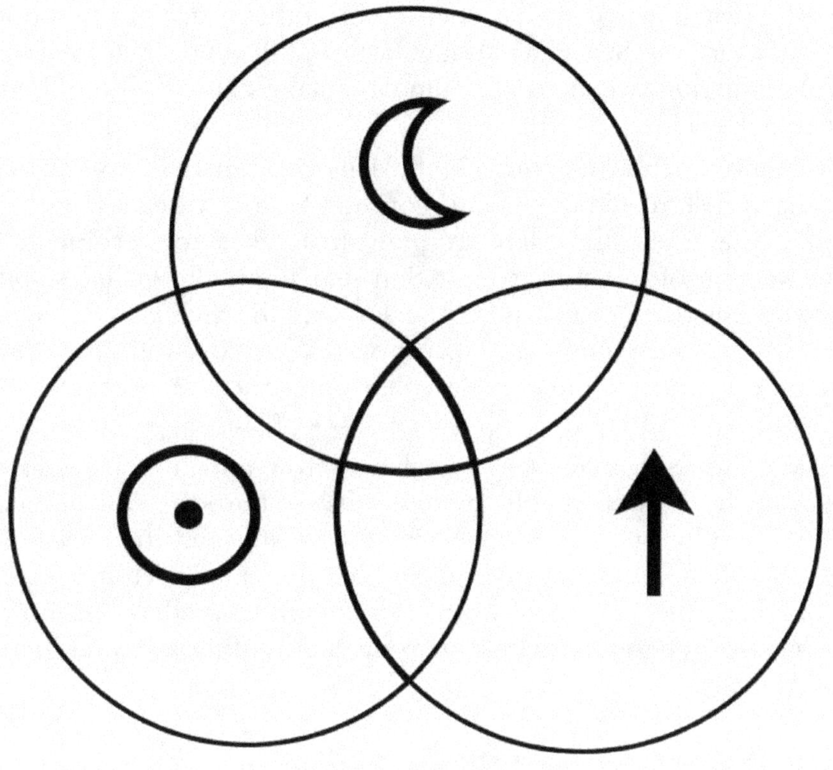

Detailed Analysis of the Sun, Moon, and Ascendant

When someone asks, "What is your sign?" they are almost always referring to the position of the Sun. However, reducing a human being to a single sign is like trying to describe a complex piece of architecture by looking only at the front door. While the Sun is vital, it is only one-third of what practitioners call "The Big Three."

To understand the core of a birth chart, you must look at the Sun, the Moon, and the Ascendant (or Rising Sign) as a unified system. Together, these three points describe your conscious will, your emotional landscape, and your physical presentation to the world.

The Sun: The Conscious Ego and Life Force

In astronomy, the Sun is the center of our solar system. It provides the light and gravitational pull that keeps every other planet in its orbit. In your birth chart, the Sun plays an identical role. It represents your central ego, your conscious will, and your fundamental identity. It is the "I am" of your personality.

If we look at the Sun through the lens of archetypal psychology, it represents the Hero's journey. This concept, famously detailed by Joseph Campbell, describes the path an individual takes to become a fully realized version of themselves. The Sun sign shows the qualities you are learning to embody. For instance, a person with the Sun in Leo is learning to embody courage and self-expression. A person with the Sun in Capricorn is learning to embody discipline and structural integrity.

It is important to note that you do not always start your life fully expressing your Sun sign. It is a goal you grow into. It represents your vitality and where you find your greatest sense of purpose. Astronomically, the Sun's position at your birth marks the season and the specific light quality of that time. As discussed in the introduction regarding chronobiology, the "season of birth" can have lasting effects on how our bodies regulate energy. The Sun in your chart is the primary symbol of that vital energy.

The Moon:
The Private Self and Emotional Safety

While the Sun represents the day, the ego, and what is visible, the Moon represents the night, the subconscious, and what is hidden. The Moon moves much faster than the Sun, changing signs every two and a half days. This rapid movement mirrors the shifting nature of our moods and emotions.

In your chart, the Moon describes how you feel, how you react instinctively, and what you need to feel safe. It is the part of you that only those closest to you—your family or long-term partners—ever truly see. If the Sun is your "spirit," the Moon is your "soul."

Psychologically, the Moon is associated with the "Inner Child." It reflects the nurturing you received in infancy and how you now nurture yourself. For example, someone with a Moon in Gemini may process emotions through talking and gathering information. They feel safe when they have intellectual variety. In contrast, someone with a Moon in Scorpio may process emotions through deep, private intensity. They feel safe when they have a sense of total honesty and emotional depth.

The relationship between your Sun and Moon is one of the most important dynamics in your chart. If they are in signs that share the same element (such as a Fire Sun and a Fire Moon), your will and your emotions tend to work in harmony. If they are in conflicting signs, you may feel a constant internal tug-of-war between what you want to achieve (Sun) and what you need to feel comfortable (Moon).

The Ascendant: The Mask and the Lens

The Ascendant, or Rising Sign, is the most specific point of the Big Three. It is the sign that was rising on the Eastern horizon at the exact minute of your birth. Because the Earth rotates so quickly, the Ascendant changes every two hours. This is why having an accurate birth time is non-negotiable for a professional reading.

The Ascendant serves two functions. First, it is the "mask" or the "persona" you show the world. It is the first impression you make on others. Second, it is the "lens" through which you view reality. If you have an Aries Ascendant, you view the world as a place of action and competition. If you have a Libra Ascendant, you view the world through the lens of relationships and balance.

Many people feel more like their Rising Sign than their Sun Sign, especially in social situations. This is because the Ascendant is the "front door" of the chart. It is how you navigate your environment. It also describes your physical appearance and your general health. In ancient astrology, the Ascendant was considered the most important point because it represents the actual physical incarnation of the person.

Synthesizing the Big Three:
The Engine, the Fuel, and the Driver

To see how these work together, we can use a simple mechanical metaphor:

- **The Sun is the Engine:** It provides the power and the core purpose.
- **The Moon is the Fuel:** It is the internal resource and the emotional state that keeps the engine running.

- **The Ascendant is the Driver:** It is the person behind the wheel who decides how the car moves through traffic and interacts with the outside world.

If you have a "driver" (Ascendant) who wants to go slow and steady, but an "engine" (Sun) that wants to race, you will experience a specific kind of life friction. Understanding these three points allows you to stop fighting your own nature. Instead of wondering why you are "socially anxious" (perhaps a Capricorn Ascendant) despite being a "natural leader" (an Aries Sun), you can recognize that both are valid parts of your structural makeup.

The Historical Perspective: The "Three Hylegs"

In medieval and Renaissance astrology, certain points in the chart were designated as *Hylegs*, or "givers of life." The Sun, the Moon, and the Ascendant were the primary candidates. Practitioners believed that the strength and health of these three points determined a person's longevity and physical constitution.

This authoritative tradition emphasizes that these are not just personality markers; they are biological markers. They were used to calculate the "Lord of the Geniture," or the planet that most strongly influenced the person's physical existence. This reminds us that astrology was historically treated with the same weight as medicine. When we look at your Big Three, we are looking at the pillars of your existence.

Mini-Workbook: Identifying Your Core Trinity

It is time to look at your own chart and record your Big Three. This is the foundation of your cosmic identity.

1. **Record Your Data:**
   - **Sun Sign:** ___________________________________

     (Your conscious identity)
   - **Moon Sign:** __________________________________

     (Your emotional needs)
   - **Ascendant Sign:** _____________________________

     (Your social mask)

2. **The Elemental Mix:** Look at the elements (Fire, Earth, Air, Water) of your Big Three.

   o   Are they the same? _______________________________

   o   Are they all different? _____________________________

   o   A mix of elements suggests a versatile personality, while a single dominant element suggests a very focused, intense temperament.

3. **The "First Impression" Exercise:** Ask a friend who doesn't know your astrology chart to describe their first impression of you in three words.

   o   **Word 1:** ____

   o   **Word 2:** ____

   o   **Word 3:** ____

   o   Do these words align more with your Ascendant sign or your Sun sign? (Often, strangers see the Ascendant first).

4. **The Midnight Check:** When you are completely alone and stressed, what is the one thing you do to feel better? (e.g., eat, clean, call a friend, hide).

   ____

   ____

   Compare this habit to the descriptions of your Moon sign. Does it match?

Chapter 3: Personal Planets

Mercury, Venus, and Mars:
Communication, Values, and Drive

While the Sun and Moon represent your core identity and emotional needs, the personal planets represent your tools for interacting with the world. Mercury, Venus, and Mars are the "inner planets" because their orbits are closest to the Sun. In a birth chart, they describe the specific mechanics of your personality. If the Sun is the "What" and the Moon is the "Why," then these three planets are the "How." They dictate how you process information, how you connect with others, and how you assert your will.

Mercury: The Architect of Thought and Speech

In mythology, Mercury was the messenger of the gods, equipped with winged sandals to move between worlds. In your chart, Mercury governs the nervous system, the hands, and the intellect. It is the planet of perception. It determines how you gather data from your environment and how you translate that data into speech or writing.

Astronomically, Mercury is never more than 28 degrees away from the Sun. This means your Mercury sign is either the same as your Sun sign or in the sign immediately preceding or following it. This proximity shows how closely our "intellect" is tied to our "identity."

From a psychological perspective, Mercury represents your cognitive style. A person with Mercury in an Earth sign like Capricorn tends to think in concrete, structured terms. They value facts and utility. Conversely, a person with Mercury in a Water sign like Cancer processes information through an emotional filter. They "feel" their way through a conversation and have a memory tied to sentiment. Understanding your Mercury placement can help you navigate communication breakdowns. You might realize that you aren't "bad at explaining things," but that you simply have a style that values detail while your partner values speed.

Venus: The Standard of Value and Attraction

Venus is often simplified as the planet of "love," but its function is much broader. In astrology, Venus represents your "valuation system." It describes what you find beautiful, what you find worth owning, and how you seek harmony. While the Moon seeks emotional safety, Venus seeks aesthetic and social pleasure.

Venus governs your "attraction factor." This is not just about romance; it is about what you are drawn to in friendship, art, and even finances. If your Venus is in an Air sign like Aquarius, you value intellectual freedom and unconventional beauty. You are attracted to people who challenge your mind. If your Venus is in a Fire sign like Aries, you value spontaneity and directness. You are attracted to the "thrill of the chase."

In social dynamics, Venus is the "peacemaker." It shows how you negotiate and how you seek to be liked. Research in social psychology regarding "attachment styles" often mirrors the functions of Venus. Just as our early social bonds dictate how we form relationships later in life, the placement of Venus in the chart acts as a blueprint for our relational habits. It shows whether we approach others with openness or with a need for self-protection.

Mars: The Engine of Desire and Conflict

If Venus is how we attract, Mars is how we pursue. Mars is the planet of energy, action, and survival. It represents the "fight or flight" response and the way we handle anger and competition. While Venus seeks to bring things together, Mars is comfortable with the separation required to win or to lead.

In your birth chart, Mars describes your "libido"—not just in a sexual sense, but as a general zest for life. It is your drive to get out of bed and accomplish a task. For example, a person with Mars in Taurus may move slowly but has incredible endurance. They are like a steamroller: hard to start, but impossible to stop once they have a goal. A person with Mars in Gemini, however, has energy that fluctuates. They are driven by variety and may start five projects at once, fueled by the excitement of the new.

Mars is also the planet of "assertion." It shows how you stand up for yourself. In the workplace, Mars determines your competitive edge. In personal life, it shows how you handle frustration. Understanding your Mars sign allows you to find healthy outlets for your physical and emotional heat. Without an outlet, "Mars energy" can turn inward, manifesting as irritability or physical tension.

The Internal Feedback Loop

These three planets form a constant feedback loop in your daily life:

1. **Mercury** notices a problem or a desire and thinks about it.
2. **Venus** decides if that thing is actually worth the effort based on your values.
3. **Mars** provides the physical energy to go out and get it or solve the problem.

When these three are in signs that conflict, you might experience "internal static." You might think one thing (Mercury), want another (Venus), and act in a way that contradicts both (Mars). This is why self-knowledge is an authoritative tool for personal management. By identifying these distinct parts of yourself, you can start to align them toward a single purpose.

Mini-Workbook: The Personal Planet Inventory

1. **Find Your Placements:**
    - **Mercury Sign:** ___________________________________
    - **Venus Sign:** ___________________________________
    - **Mars Sign:** ___________________________________
2. **The "Learning Style" Check:** Based on your Mercury sign, are you a visual, auditory, or kinesthetic learner?
    - Example: Mercury in Air signs often prefer reading/talking (auditory/verbal); Mercury in Earth signs often prefer doing (kinesthetic).
    - **My Learning Style:** ___________________________________
    ____
3. **The "Value" Prompt:** List three things you cannot live without in a relationship (e.g., humor, reliability, passion).
    1. ___________________________________
    2. ___________________________________
    3. ___________________________________
    How do these three things reflect the qualities of your Venus sign?

    ____

    ____

    ____

    ____
4. **The "Energy" Log:** When do you feel most productive during the day?

    ____

    ____

    Look at your Mars sign's element. Fire/Air signs often have "burst" energy; Earth/Water signs often have "steady" or "cyclical" energy.

Chapter 4: Social and Outer Planets

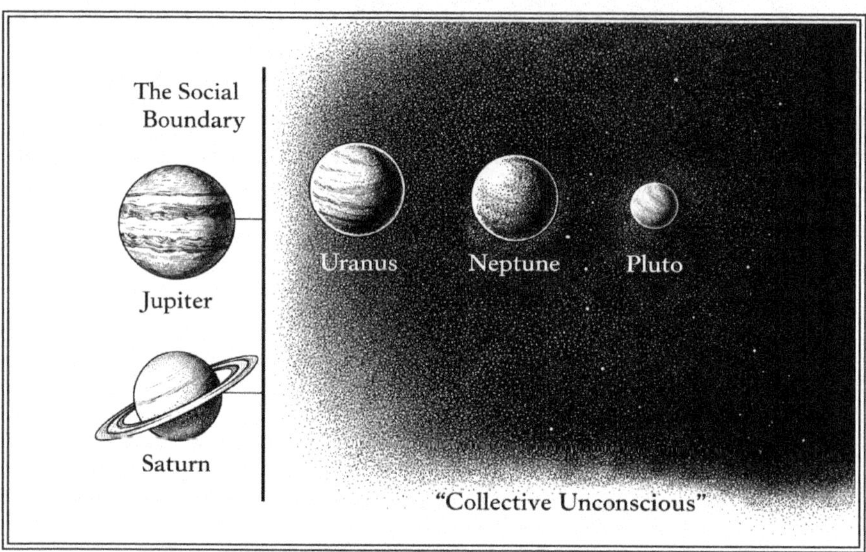

From Jupiter's Growth to Pluto's Transformation

While the inner planets, Mercury, Venus, and Mars, describe your personal habits and daily choices, the social and outer planets describe your relationship to the world at large. These five celestial bodies, Jupiter, Saturn, Uranus, Neptune, and Pluto, represent the forces that are often beyond our immediate control. They represent the "climate" of your life rather than the "weather." Understanding these placements helps you see how you fit into your specific generation and how you handle the larger cycles of growth and change.

The Social Bridge: Jupiter and Saturn

Jupiter and Saturn are known as the social planets because they bridge the gap between the individual and the collective. They represent the two primary ways we interact with social structures: through expansion and through discipline.

Jupiter: The Principle of Expansion and Belief

Jupiter is the largest planet in our solar system. In astrology, its function is equally vast. It represents your "expansion point." Jupiter describes how you seek to grow, where you find meaning, and how you experience luck. Because it stays in a zodiac sign for about one year, it colors the "flavor" of success for everyone born in that twelve-month period.

Psychologically, Jupiter represents your "optimism bias." It is the part of you that believes everything will work out. However, Jupiter is not just about blind faith; it is about the search for truth. A person with Jupiter in a Fire sign like Sagittarius may find growth through travel and risk-taking. They believe the world is fundamentally a place of abundance. A person with Jupiter in an Earth sign like Virgo may find growth through mastery of craft and attention to detail. For them, "luck" is the result of being extremely well-prepared. Jupiter shows where you are naturally generous and where you seek the "big picture."

Astronomically, Jupiter acts as a celestial vacuum cleaner. Its massive gravity pulls in asteroids and comets that might otherwise strike Earth. Symbolically, this mirrors its astrological role: it "protects" us by providing a sense of hope and a broader perspective that keeps us from getting bogged down in the minutiae of daily struggles.

Saturn: The Principle of Contraction and Structure

If Jupiter is the "Yes" of the cosmos, Saturn is the "No." In traditional astrology, Saturn was known as the "Great Malefic," but modern practitioners view it more as a "Great Teacher." It represents boundaries, time, discipline, and the reality principle. Saturn describes where you feel inadequate and, consequently, where you must work the hardest.

Saturn stays in a sign for about two and a half years. Its placement shows where you face your greatest fears. However, this is also where you can achieve your greatest mastery. If Saturn is in your 2nd House of money, you may face financial struggles early in life, but these very challenges will likely force you to become an expert in financial management. Saturn requires effort, but it pays in "dividends" of long-term stability.

The discovery of Saturn's rings in the 17th century added a layer of symbolism to the planet. The rings represent the "limits" of the visible world. Before the invention of the telescope, Saturn was the furthest planet known to man. It represented the boundary of human experience. This is why Saturn is still associated with the "limitations" of time and physical reality.

The Transpersonal Trio: The Generational Markers

Uranus, Neptune, and Pluto are invisible to the naked eye. They were discovered in modern times (1781, 1846, and 1930, respectively) and are called the "transpersonal" planets. Because they move so slowly—Pluto can take up to 20 years to move through a single sign—they describe the shared experiences of an entire generation. They represent the collective unconscious and the slow, deep shifts in human history.

Uranus: The Rebel and the Innovator

Uranus represents sudden change, revolution, and the breaking of old patterns. It is the planet of the "Aha!" moment. In your chart, the house position of Uranus shows where you are most likely to be unconventional or eccentric. It is where you feel a need for total freedom.

The history of Uranus's discovery coincides with the American and French Revolutions. It shattered the "limit" set by Saturn, showing that there was more to the universe than what had been known for millennia. This is why Uranus is associated with radical shifts in thought. If Uranus is in your 4th House of home, your family life may be unusual or you may move frequently. Uranus serves to wake us up from complacency. It is the lightning bolt that strikes when a situation has become too rigid.

Neptune: The Dreamer and the Mystic

Neptune represents the dissolution of boundaries. It is the planet of art, spirituality, and illusion. While Saturn builds walls and Uranus breaks them, Neptune melts them. In your chart, Neptune shows where you are most sensitive and where you might experience confusion or escapism.

Neptune was discovered through mathematical prediction before it was ever seen through a lens. This perfectly mirrors its astrological nature: it represents that which we "feel" but cannot always see. It is the source of your imagination and your connection to the divine or the collective "oneness." A person with a strong Neptune might be a gifted artist or healer, but they must be careful to stay grounded in physical reality. Without a strong Saturn to provide structure, Neptune's dreams can become delusions or a way to hide from the harshness of the world.

Pluto: The Alchemist and the Power Broker

Pluto is the planet of "death and rebirth." It represents the deep, hidden power within the psyche. Pluto's influence is subtle but total. It shows where you experience power struggles and where you must undergo a complete "shedding of skin" at some point in your life.

Pluto was discovered during the rise of psychoanalysis and the discovery of nuclear fission. This dual nature, the power of the hidden mind and the power of the split atom, defines Pluto's energy. It is about the process of taking something raw and turning it into something refined through intense pressure. In your chart, Pluto marks the area where you are forced to evolve. You cannot negotiate with Pluto; you can only surrender to the transformation it demands.

The Interplay of Growth and Discipline

The balance between Jupiter and Saturn is the most practical part of this chapter. Most people suffer because they are "lopsided" in this area.

- **The Over-Jupitered Individual:** This person has many big ideas but lacks the discipline to finish them. They are always chasing the next "lucky break" but never build a foundation.

- **The Over-Saturned Individual:** This person is incredibly hard-working but lacks the vision to take a risk. They are so afraid of making a mistake that they stay in situations that no longer serve them.

The goal is to use your Jupiter "vision" to find your path and your Saturn "discipline" to walk it. In your workbook section, you will analyze how these two planets interact in your own life to find your personal "middle ground."

Generational Astrology:
The Outer Planet Cycles

When we look at the outer planets, we are looking at the "mood" of a generation. For example, the "Baby Boomers" mostly have Pluto in Leo, a sign associated with self-expression and individual authority. This generation transformed the way we view the self. Generation X has Pluto in Libra, a sign of relationships and justice, leading to shifts in how we view marriage and social contracts. Millennials have Pluto in Scorpio, the sign of deep psychology and hidden truths, which explains their focus on mental health and transparency.

By understanding your generational markers (Uranus, Neptune, and Pluto), you can see how your personal life is a piece of a much larger historical puzzle. You aren't just an individual; you are a representative of a specific "wave" of human evolution.

Mini-Workbook: Social and Outer Analysis

1. **Identify Your Placements:**

    o **Jupiter Sign:** ___________________________________
       (Where I find growth)

    o **Saturn Sign:** ___________________________________
       (Where I face my fears/work hard)

    o **Uranus Sign:** __________________________________
       (My generational "innovation" sign)

    o **Neptune Sign:** _________________________________
       (My generational "dream" sign)

    o **Pluto Sign:** ___________________________________
       (My generational "power" sign)

2. **The Saturn Challenge:** Look at the house where your Saturn is located. List one area of that life sector (e.g., career, relationship, health) that has always felt "difficult" or "slow" for you.

    ____

    ____

3. **The Jupiter Opportunity:** Look at the house where your Jupiter is located. Where do things seem to "just work out" for you with minimal effort?

    ____

    ____

4. **Generational Connection:** Look up the years for your Uranus and Neptune signs. Do most of your friends share these signs? How do you see your generation's shared "dream" (Neptune) manifesting in current social trends?

    ____

    ____

Chapter 5: Aspects and Geometry

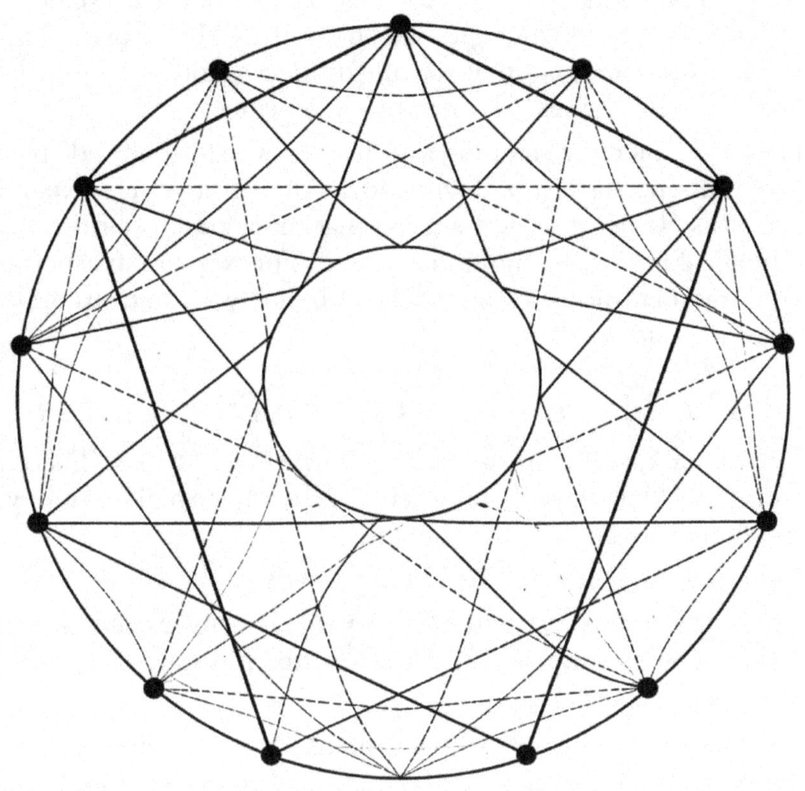

How Angles Create Internal Tension or Ease

If the planets are the actors and the houses are the stages, then the aspects are the script. Aspects are the mathematical angles that planets form with one another as they move around the 360-degree circle of the zodiac. These angles determine how your internal "players" communicate. Some planets speak to each other with ease and support, while others speak through friction, challenge, and tension. This geometry is what gives a birth chart its depth; it explains why you might have a "strong" Sun but still feel hesitant to lead, or why your emotional Moon feels at odds with your logical Mercury.

The Harmonic Basis of Astrology

The study of aspects is rooted in the same principles as musical harmony. The ancient mathematician Pythagoras believed that the universe was built on numerical ratios, a concept known as the "Music of the Spheres." When two planets are placed at specific distances from each other, such as 90 degrees or 120 degrees, they create a "resonance."

Johannes Kepler, the famous astronomer who discovered the laws of planetary motion, was also a deep student of astrology. He expanded the system of aspects because he believed that the geometry of the sky had a direct, physical impact on the human spirit. For Kepler, an aspect was not "magic"; it was a harmonic resonance, much like two piano strings vibrating together when one is struck.

The Major Aspects: The Five Voices

In this workbook, we focus on the five "Ptolemaic" aspects. These are the primary angles that have been used for nearly two thousand years to interpret the "dialogue" between planets.

1. The Conjunction (0°): The Unified Voice

A conjunction occurs when two planets are sitting right next to each other. Their energies merge so completely that it is hard to tell where one ends and the other begins.

- **The Experience:** This is an intense, concentrated energy. If you have the Sun conjunct Mars, your identity (Sun) and your drive (Mars) are one. You don't "think" about being brave; you simply act.

- **The Challenge:** Because the energies are fused, you may lack perspective. It can be hard to see these traits objectively because they are so central to your being.

2. The Sextile (60°): The Supportive Conversation

A sextile occurs when planets are two signs apart. This is a "soft" aspect that represents opportunity and talent.

- **The Experience:** This is like a friendly suggestion. It provides a spark of creativity or a helpful connection. However, unlike other aspects, the sextile requires your effort. It is an "invitation" that you must choose to accept.

- **The Challenge:** Because it is so easy, you might take this talent for granted and fail to develop it.

3. The Square (90°): The Productive Friction

The square is a "hard" aspect that occurs when planets are three signs apart. This creates a state of internal tension.

- **The Experience:** This feels like a "tug-of-war." For example, if your Moon (emotion) is square your Mercury (logic), you might feel that your feelings and your thoughts are constantly interrupting each other.

- **The Productive Side:** Friction creates heat, and heat creates movement. People with many squares in their charts are often high achievers because the internal tension forces them to take action and solve problems.

4. The Trine (120°): The Harmonious Flow

The trine occurs when planets are four signs apart, usually in the same element (Fire to Fire, Earth to Earth, etc.).

- **The Experience:** This is the easiest aspect. Energy flows between the two planets without any resistance. It represents natural gifts and "innate" luck.

- **The Challenge:** Because there is no tension, trines can lead to laziness. If life is too easy in one area, you may never feel the need to grow or change.

5. The Opposition (180°): The Mirror

An opposition occurs when planets are directly across the wheel from each other.

- **The Experience:** This feels like a "see-saw." You may feel like you are oscillating between two extremes. For instance, an opposition between Venus (values) and Mars (action) might manifest as a struggle between wanting peace and wanting to fight.

- **The Solution:** Oppositions require "integration." The goal is to find the middle ground where both planets can exist together, rather than choosing one over the other.

The Concept of Orbs: The Range of Influence

Planets do not have to be at the *exact* degree to form an aspect. Astrologers use a "range" known as an **Orb**. For example, if two planets are 92 degrees apart, they are still considered to be "in square" because they are within the acceptable range (usually 8 to 10 degrees).

The "tighter" the orb (the closer the planets are to the exact number), the more powerful the aspect will be in your life. A square with a 1-degree orb will be a dominant theme in your personality, while a square with an 8-degree orb might be a subtle background hum.

Chart Patterns: The Geometry of the Soul

When multiple aspects connect, they form geometric shapes within the chart. These are known as "Aspect Patterns."

- **The Grand Trine:** An equilateral triangle formed by three planets. This indicates a high level of natural talent and self-sufficiency.

- **The T-Square:** Two planets in opposition, both forming a square to a third planet. This creates a "focal point" of intense pressure that often leads to great accomplishment.

- **The Stellium:** A cluster of three or more planets in a single sign or house. This indicates a massive concentration of energy in one specific area of life.

Psychological Integration:
Owning Your Geometry

In the framework of archetypal psychology, aspects show us where our "inner sub-personalities" are in conflict. A square between Saturn and the Sun might manifest as a "harsh inner critic." By recognizing this as a geometric relationship in your chart, you can begin to externalize the critic. It is not "you" who is the problem; it is a specific dialogue between your need for structure (Saturn) and your need for expression (Sun). This perspective allows for a more compassionate and objective approach to self-improvement.

Mini-Workbook: The Dialogue of Your Planets

To complete this section, look at the "Aspect Table" or the "Lines" in the center of your birth chart.

1. **Find One Trine (120°):**

    List the two planets involved. _______________ and ___________

    What is one natural talent you have that combines these two energies? (e.g., if Mercury trines Jupiter, you might be a natural storyteller).

    ____

    ____

2. **Find One Square (90°):**

    List the two planets involved. _______________ and ___________

    What is a recurring "internal argument" you have with yourself? How do these two planets represent that argument?

    ____

    ____

3. **The Tightest Aspect:** Look for the aspect with the smallest "Orb" (the number closest to zero). Which two planets are they? ___________ and ___________

    This is likely the most active "voice" in your personality.

4. **Pattern Check:** Does your chart have any large geometric shapes (triangles, squares, or clusters)? List them here.

    ____

    ____

Conclusion: Synthesizing the Data into a Cohesive Snapshot

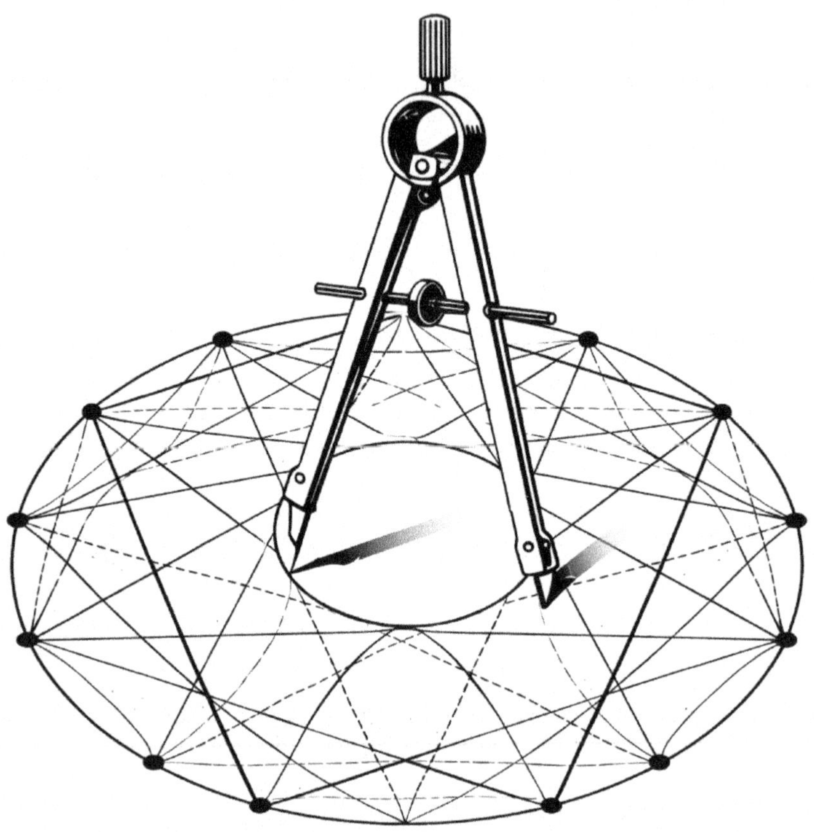

You have spent the previous chapters dismantling your birth chart, examining its individual gears and springs. You have looked at the "Big Three" as separate pillars, dissected the personal tools of Mercury, Venus, and Mars, felt the social weight of Jupiter and Saturn, and traced the geometric lines of your aspects. However, a person is not a list of separate parts. You are a living, breathing system where all these forces interact simultaneously. Synthesis is the art of "Chart Judgment": the process of looking at the map not as a collection of data points, but as a unified story.

The Art of the Holistic View

In the early days of astrology, practitioners often struggled with what they called "contradictory testimonies." For example, a chart might show a very brave Mars but a very fearful Saturn. Ancient astrologers like Vettius Valens sought to find the "Lord of the Chart", the single planet that held the most power, to resolve these contradictions. Today, we call this synthesis. We understand that humans are complex enough to hold two opposing truths at once.

Synthesis requires you to look for the "dominant themes" rather than getting lost in every minor detail. If you see three different placements that point toward a love of communication (perhaps Mercury in the 1st House, the Sun in Gemini, and a strong 3rd House), that theme is "loud." It is a primary color in your life. If you have one small placement that suggests you are shy, it doesn't mean the chart is wrong; it means that shyness is a subtle "tint" rather than a main feature.

The Three Layers of Synthesis

To create a cohesive snapshot of your data, professional astrologers use a layered approach. You can follow this same method to summarize your findings:

1. **The Landscape (The Hemispheres and Elements):** Look at where the planets are grouped. Are they mostly in the top half (Public) or the bottom half (Private)? Is there a heavy concentration of Fire, Earth, Air, or Water? This gives you the "vibe" or the "environment" of the person before you even read a single sign.

2. **The Core Trinity (Sun, Moon, Ascendant):** This is the heart of the engine. If these three are in harmony, the person moves through life with a sense of internal consistency. If they are in conflict, life is a series of internal negotiations. This is the "who" of the story.

3. **The Aspect Web (The Dynamics):** The lines you see in the center of the chart show the "how." They show where the core trinity gets help and where it meets resistance. A square from Saturn to the Sun might mean the identity is forged through hard work and overcoming self-doubt. A trine from Jupiter to the Moon might mean the emotional life is naturally resilient and hopeful.

Moving from Information to Wisdom

The goal of "unlocking" your chart is not just to collect facts about yourself. It is to gain a bird's-eye view of your own life path. When you synthesize your data, you stop seeing your challenges as "bad luck" and start seeing them as the necessary friction required to build your specific character.

Consider the work of James Hillman, a psychologist who developed "The Acorn Theory." He argued that each person comes into the world with a "daimon" or a unique blueprint—much like an acorn contains the entire pattern of the oak tree it will become. The birth chart is that blueprint. By synthesizing the data, you are looking at the "oak tree" version of yourself. You are seeing the potential of what you can become if you work *with* your natural energies instead of against them.

As you close this first book, you should have a "working statement" of your identity. This isn't a final verdict, but a grounded starting point. You are a complex individual, and your chart is a high-resolution map of that complexity. In the next book, we will move from these structural foundations into the deep psychological meanings of the Zodiac signs themselves, exploring the "Twelve Archetypes of the Human Soul."

Synthesis Exercise: The One-Sentence Snapshot

The most powerful way to synthesize your Book 1 data is to fill in the following authoritative statement. This forces your brain to prioritize the most important parts of your chart.

"I am an individual driven by [Sun Sign's Purpose], who processes life through a lens of [Ascendant Sign's Style], and finds emotional security in [Moon Sign's Environment]."

Example: "I am an individual driven by meticulous service (Sun in Virgo), who processes life through a lens of intense investigation (Scorpio Rising), and finds emotional security in intellectual variety (Moon in Gemini)."

Reflection Questions: Assessing Your Initial Reactions to Your Chart

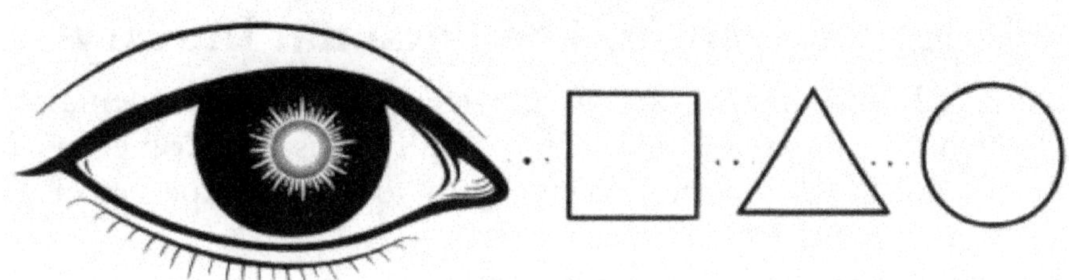

Now that you have plotted your planets, identified your houses, and traced the geometric lines of your aspects, you are looking at a finished map of your psyche. For many, this is a profound moment of "recognition." You are seeing patterns that you have felt your entire life finally given a name and a place. For others, the initial reaction might be one of confusion or even resistance. Both reactions are equally valid and important for the process of self-discovery.

The birth chart acts as a mirror. If you don't recognize the reflection, it may be because you have spent years suppressing certain parts of your nature to fit into societal or familial expectations. Alternatively, you may be focusing on a "shadow" version of a placement rather than its potential. These reflection questions are designed to help you sift through your data and find the personal truth within the technical symbols.

The Psychological Mirror: Identification and Resistance

In the practice of analytical psychology, we often talk about the "Persona" (the face we show the world) and the "Shadow" (the parts of ourselves we deny). Your birth chart contains both.

- **Identification:** This happens when you read a description and feel an immediate "Yes, that is exactly me." This usually occurs with your "Big Three" or heavily populated houses.

- **Resistance:** This happens when you look at a placement and think, "That doesn't sound like me at all." This resistance is often where the most growth happens. It may indicate a talent you haven't dared to use yet, or a trait you've been taught to hide.

As you work through these questions, be radically honest with yourself. There are no right or wrong answers. This is about the conversation between you and your cosmic blueprint.

Deep Reflection: The Personal Inquiry

1. The "Aha" Moment Look at your completed House Identification Log. Which specific area of life (e.g., the 4th House of Home, the 10th House of Career) felt the most "accurate" to your lived experience? Why did seeing it on paper feel like a relief?

Your Response:

____

____

____

2. The Disconnect Is there a planet or sign in your chart that feels like a "stranger" to you? For example, if you have a lot of planets in Fire signs but perceive yourself as a quiet, cautious person. Explore this gap. Is it possible you are suppressing this energy, or are you expressing it in a way you hadn't realized?

Your Response:

____

____

____

3. The Strength of the Angles Think about your Ascendant (the 1st House cusp). This is how you "start" things. When you walk into a room of strangers or start a new project, does your behavior match the sign on your Ascendant? If not, what "mask" are you wearing instead?

Your Response:

____

____

____

4. The Hidden Gifts Look at your "Blue Lines" (Trines and Sextiles). These are your natural talents. Often, we ignore these because they come so easily to us that we assume everyone can do them. What is one thing you do effortlessly that others seem to struggle with? How does this relate to your trines?

Your Response:

----

5. The Friction Points Look at your "Red Lines" (Squares and Oppositions). These represent internal tension. Instead of seeing them as "bad," try to describe the *benefit* of this tension. For example, if your Mercury (Mind) is square Saturn (Restriction), the "friction" might make you an incredibly careful and precise thinker. What is the hidden "superpower" in your greatest internal conflict?

Your Response:

The "One Word" Synthesis

If you had to choose one word to describe the "theme" of your birth chart based on what you've learned in Book 1, what would it be? (Examples: *Communication, Stability, Transformation, Service, Exploration*).

My Theme:

Workbook Section 1:
The Chart Blueprint

In this section, you move from theory to application. You will record the specific data that makes your birth chart a unique astronomical document. By writing these details down, you "lock in" the foundations of your cosmic identity, creating a reference point you can return to whenever you feel lost or overwhelmed by the complexity of astrological symbols.

Part 1: The Birth Data Log

Before plotting your chart, ensure you have the most accurate data possible. As discussed in the introduction, even a few minutes can change your House cusps.

- **Full Name:** ____
- **Birth Date:** ____
- **Birth Time:** ____
- **Birth Location (City, State/Country):** ____________________
- **Latitude/Longitude (Optional):** __________________________

Part 2: The House Identification Log

The Houses represent the "stage" where your life plays out. Look at your generated birth chart and record the sign that is on the **Cusp** (the starting line) of each house.

1. House 1 (The Self/Appearance): ____________________________
2. House 2 (Personal Resources/Money): _______________________
3. House 3 (Communication/Siblings): _________________________
4. House 4 (Home/Roots): _____________________________________
5. House 5 (Creativity/Children): ____________________________
6. House 6 (Work/Health): ____________________________________
7. House 7 (Partnerships/Open Others): _______________________
8. House 8 (Shared Resources/Transformation): ________________
9. House 9 (Philosophy/Travel): ______________________________
10. House 10 (Career/Public Reputation): _____________________

11. House 11 (Friendships/Groups): ___________________________

12. House 12 (Subconscious/Retreat): ________________________

Part 3: The Planetary Inventory

List your planets, their signs, and their specific degrees. The degree (from 0° to 29°) is vital for calculating the "Aspects" or conversations between the planets.

Planet	Symbol	Sign	Degree (0°-29°)	House Number
Sun	☉			
Moon	☽			
Mercury	☿			
Venus	♀			
Mars	♂			
Jupiter	♃			
Saturn	♄			
Uranus	♅			
Neptune	♆			
Pluto	♇			
Ascendant	AC			(Always House 1)

Part 4: The Aspect Tracker

List the three "Tightest" (most exact) aspects in your chart. Look for the smallest "Orb" numbers on your chart's aspect grid.

1. **Planet:** _______________________

   Aspect: _______________________

   Planet: _______________________

   (Orb: _______________________)

2. **Planet:** _______________________

   Aspect: _______________________

   Planet: _______________________

   (Orb: _______________________)

3. **Planet:** _______________________

   Aspect: _______________________

   Planet: _______________________

   (Orb: _______________________)

Part 5: Synthesis Summary

Based on your plotting above, answer these three grounding questions:

1. **Elemental Dominance:** Which element appears most in your chart? (Fire, Earth, Air, Water)

   ____

   ____

2. **Hemisphere Emphasis:** Are most of your planets in the top half (Public) or bottom half (Private) of the wheel?

   ____

   ____

3. **The Dominant House:** Which house has the most planets clustered inside it? (This is your "Stellium" or area of greatest life focus).

   ____

   ____

BOOK TWO
Discover Your Cosmic Identity

Introduction: Moving Beyond "Sun Sign" Stereotypes

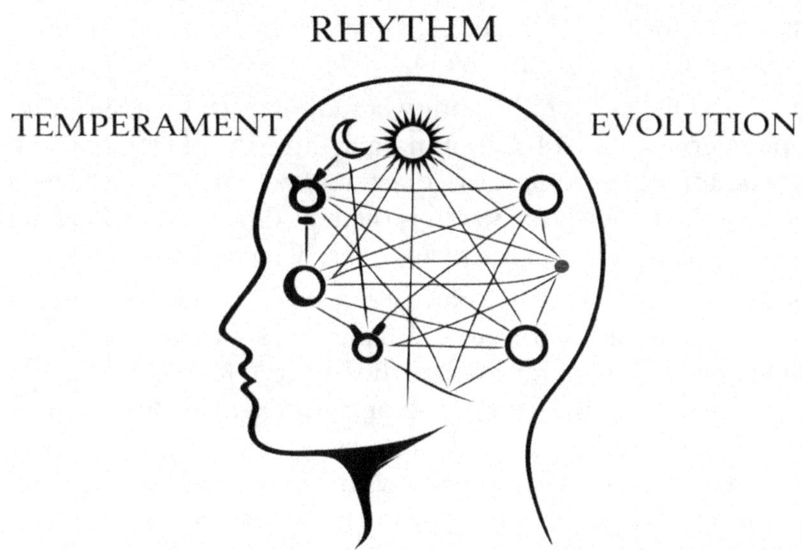

The Crisis of the Over-Simplified Self

If you have spent any time in the modern world, you have likely encountered the "Twelve Tribe" version of astrology. This is the version found in the back of glossy magazines or in catchy social media headlines that claim all Scorpios are vengeful, all Taureans are lazy, or all Geminis are two-faced. While these stereotypes are often rooted in a grain of archetypal truth, they are the "fast food" of astrological knowledge. They provide immediate recognition but offer no long-term psychological nourishment.

The primary goal of Book 2 is to move you beyond these flat, two-dimensional caricatures. When we rely solely on the Sun sign to define ourselves, we ignore the staggering complexity of the human psyche. You are not a monolith; you are an ecosystem. In the first book, we built the skeleton of your chart: the houses and the planetary positions. Now, we must put flesh on those bones. We must understand how the different "frequencies" of your chart interact to create the specific, nuanced person you are today.

The Historical Shift: From Fate to Character

To understand why we need to move beyond stereotypes, we must look at how astrology has evolved. For the better part of two thousand years, astrology was primarily "event-oriented." It was used to predict if a king would win a war or if a merchant's ship would return from sea. In this "External Astrology," the nuances of a person's inner feelings were secondary to the "Fate" that awaited them.

However, in the early 20th century, a radical shift occurred. Influenced by the pioneering work of Carl Jung and the rise of depth psychology, astrology began to move inward. Practitioners began to realize that the "Fate" we meet in the external world is often just the outward manifestation of our internal character. As the saying goes, "Character is destiny."

This shift turned the birth chart into a tool for self-actualization. We stopped looking at the Sun sign as a "label" and started looking at it as a "core potential." If you are a Leo who doesn't feel bold, the modern astrologer doesn't say the chart is wrong. Instead, we look at the other layers. Perhaps your "Fire" is being dampened by an overwhelming amount of "Earth" in your temperament, or perhaps your "Fixed" nature is making you resistant to the very self-expression your Sun sign craves.

The Three Foundations of Nuance

In this book, we will explore three foundational layers that explain why you might feel different from the "standard" description of your sign. These layers provide the texture and the "shading" of your personality.

1. The Elemental Temperament

Long before modern personality tests like the Myers-Briggs or the Enneagram, there were the Four Elements. Fire, Earth, Air, and Water are the "fuel" of the human machine. If the Sun is the "driver," the elements are what's in the tank. We will learn how to calculate your elemental balance to see if you are naturally driven by inspiration, logic, feeling, or physical reality. This layer explains your energy levels and your basic "vibe" that others pick up on before you even speak.

2. The Modalities: Your Approach to Movement

Have you ever wondered why some people are great at starting projects but terrible at finishing them? Or why some people can endure anything but refuse to change direction? This is the work of the **Modalities**

(Cardinal, Fixed, and Mutable). This layer describes your relationship with change and time. By identifying your dominant modality, you can stop fighting your natural rhythm and start working with it.

3. The Evolutionary Points (Nodes and Chiron)

Finally, we move into the "Soul's Journey." Your identity is not static; it is evolving. We will examine the **Lunar Nodes**, which act as a compass for your life path, and **Chiron**, the "Wounded Healer," which points to the recurring challenges that eventually become your greatest strengths. This is where we move from "Who am I?" to "Who am I becoming?"

The Psychological Concept of "Individuation"

Carl Jung coined the term "Individuation" to describe the process of becoming the person you were always meant to be: of integrating the various, often conflicting parts of your psyche into a whole. The birth chart is the ultimate map for this process.

Most people experience a "Split Identity." They have a public self (the Ascendant), a conscious ego (the Sun), and a private, emotional self (the Moon). Often, these three are at odds. You might have a "Mutable" Moon that wants to go with the flow, but a "Cardinal" Sun that wants to take charge. This internal friction is not a flaw; it is the "grit" in the oyster that creates the pearl.

In this book, we are looking for your **Signature Sign.** This is a technical calculation that identifies the one zodiac sign that summarizes your elemental and modal balance. For many people, their Signature Sign is *different* from their Sun sign. Discovering this can be a "eureka" moment, it provides the missing piece of the puzzle that explains why you feel like a "hybrid" rather than a purebred version of your sign.

The Danger of Archetypal Literalism

One of the biggest hurdles in modern astrology is "Literalism"—the belief that if you have a certain placement, you *must* act a certain way. An authoritative approach to astrology rejects this.

Instead, we view the signs and planets as **Archetypes.** An archetype is a universal pattern of energy. "The Warrior" is an archetype. How that warrior shows up in your life depends on your culture, your upbringing, and your personal choices. One person might express their "Mars" energy by being a professional athlete; another might express it by being a fierce advocate for social justice. The "energy" is the same, but the "manifestation" is unique.

By the end of this book, you will have a more sophisticated vocabulary for describing your internal world. You will be able to move beyond the shallow water of "I am a Libra" and into the deep ocean of "I am an Air-dominant individual with a Cardinal drive, navigating a lifelong lesson in balance and self-assertion."

Mini-Workbook: Deconstructing the Label

This exercise is designed to help you see the "layers" of your identity that have been hidden behind your Sun sign.

1. **The "Expectation" List:** List three traits people *expect* you to have because of your Sun sign.

    ____

    ____

    ____

2. **The "Hidden" Reality:** For each trait above, write down how you *actually* feel or behave.

    ____

    ____

    ____

3. **The "Archetype" Connection:** Look at the traits you *actually* possess. Do they feel more like "Fire" (passion), "Earth" (reliability), "Air" (curiosity), or "Water" (emotion)?

    ____

    ____

    ____

Chapter 1: The Four Elements

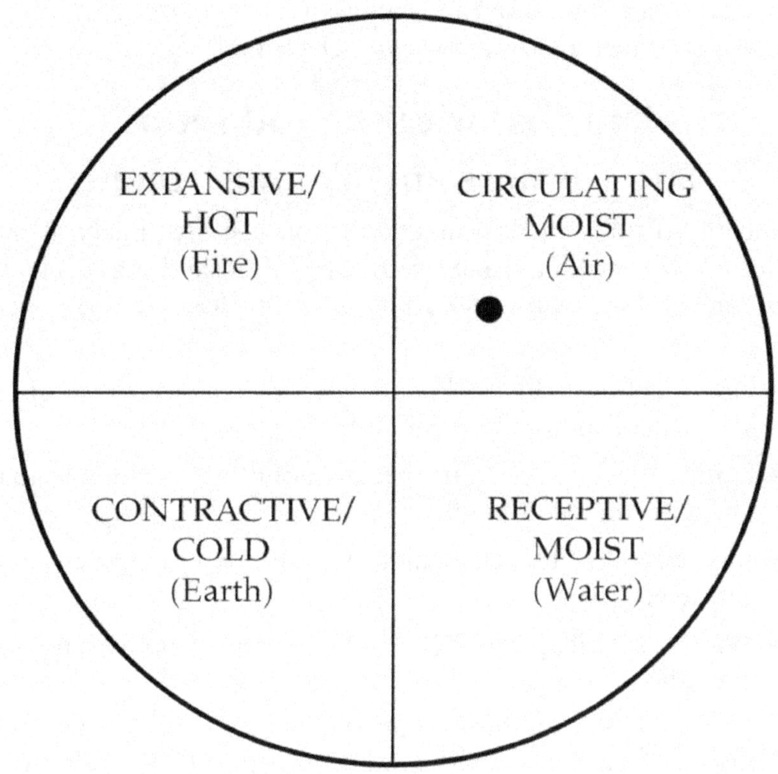

The Energetic States of Matter and Mind

In the modern world, we categorize reality through the periodic table of elements: a complex list of atomic weights and chemical properties. However, for most of human history, the world was understood through four primary "states" of being: Fire, Earth, Air, and Water. In the 5th century BCE, the philosopher Empedocles proposed that these four "roots" were the building blocks of all life. In your birth chart, these elements represent your **psychological fuel.** They describe your basic temperament, your metabolic energy levels, and the specific "lens" through which you perceive reality.

While your Sun sign tells us about your conscious identity, your **Elemental Balance** tells us about your constitutional makeup. This is the "humoral" theory of the body, once used by ancient physicians like

Hippocrates to diagnose physical and mental health. If you have a chart dominated by Water, you will experience life primarily through feelings and intuition, regardless of whether your Sun is in a logical sign like Gemini. Understanding these ratios allows you to see why you might feel "suffocated" in certain environments and "electrified" in others.

The Historical Foundation: The Humors and Temperament

The concept of the four elements is not just "spiritual"; it was the foundation of Western medicine for over two thousand years. The Greeks believed that the four elements corresponded to four "humors" or bodily fluids:

- **Fire** (Yellow Bile): The Choleric temperament—ambitious, leader-like, and easily angered.

- **Earth** (Black Bile): The Melancholic temperament—analytical, quiet, and detail-oriented.

- **Air** (Blood): The Sanguine temperament—social, lively, and talkative.

- **Water** (Phlegm): The Phlegmatic temperament—calm, empathetic, and reliable.

When we look at your birth chart, we are looking at the "recipe" of these humors. A balanced individual was thought to have a relatively equal distribution of these forces. However, most of us are "tilted" toward one or two. This tilt isn't a flaw; it is your specific specialty. It is the reason why some people are naturally designed to be pioneers (Fire), builders (Earth), messengers (Air), or healers (Water).

Deep Dive: The Four Elemental Profiles

To truly understand your "Cosmic Identity," we must look at how these elements function as internal states of matter.

Fire: The Radiant Energy (Aries, Leo, Sagittarius)

Fire is the only element that provides its own light. Astronomically, it corresponds to the plasma state. In your psyche, Fire represents the **Will**. It is the spark of inspiration that moves you to act before you have even thought the process through.

- **The Psychological Function:** Intuition and Spirit. Fire types "know" things instantly. They operate on gut feelings and a sense of destiny.

- **In the World:** They are the initiators. They thrive on challenge and become depressed when life becomes too routine or predictable.

- **The Shadow:** "The Scorched Earth." When Fire is out of balance, it becomes impulsive, ego-driven, and insensitive to the slower, softer needs of others.

- **The Fuel:** Fire is recharged by physical movement, creative risks, and the heat of competition.

Earth: The Material Reality (Taurus, Virgo, Capricorn)

Earth corresponds to the solid state of matter. It is the element of the physical senses. While Fire is about the "Idea," Earth is about the "Manifestation." It is the most "real" of the elements.

- **The Psychological Function:** Sensation and Utility. Earth types perceive the world through what they can touch, taste, and measure. They value stability and the slow, steady growth of a project.

- **In the World:** They are the providers and the architects. They keep the world running by attending to the logistics that others ignore.

- **The Shadow:** "The Heavy Stone." Excess Earth leads to a lack of imagination, a fear of change, and a tendency to become a slave to routine and material security.

- **The Fuel:** Earth is recharged by contact with nature, gardening, physical touch, and the satisfaction of a completed task.

Air: The Intellectual Breath (Gemini, Libra, Aquarius)

Air corresponds to the gaseous state. It is the only element that can circulate freely, connecting distant points. In your psyche, Air represents the **Mind.** It is the element of objectivity and social cohesion.

- **The Psychological Function:** Thinking and Perspective. Air types need to step back from a situation to understand it. They process life through concepts, words, and social interaction.

- **In the World:** They are the bridge-builders. They translate complex ideas into common language and thrive in environments where information is constantly flowing.

- **The Shadow:** "The Dissipated Cloud." Too much Air leads to indecision, emotional coldness, and a "head-in-the-clouds" existence where nothing ever touches the ground.

- **The Fuel:** Air is recharged by conversation, reading, wide-open spaces, and mental puzzles.

Water: The Emotional Depth (Cancer, Scorpio, Pisces)

Water corresponds to the liquid state. It has no shape of its own; it takes the shape of whatever container it is in. In your psyche, Water represents the **Soul.** It is the element of empathy, memory, and the unconscious.

- **The Psychological Function:** Feeling and Absorption. Water types don't "think" about the world; they "absorb" it. They are hyper-aware of the emotional undertones in any room.

- **In the World:** They are the nurturers and the visionaries. They provide the emotional glue that holds families and communities together.

- **The Shadow:** "The Raging Flood." Unbalanced Water leads to moodiness, becoming a "psychic sponge" for others' problems, and getting lost in the past.

- **The Fuel:** Water is recharged by solitude, proximity to actual bodies of water, music, and deep, intimate connection.

The Mechanics of Elemental Balance: How to Calculate Your Score

To move beyond the Sun sign, we use a weighted point system. This is an authoritative method used by professional astrologers to find your "Elemental Signature." Refer back to your **Planetary Inventory** from Book 1.

The Weighting System:

1. **Sun, Moon, and Ascendant:** 3 Points Each (The Core)
2. **Mercury, Venus, and Mars:** 2 Points Each (The Personal Tools)
3. **Jupiter and Saturn:** 1 Point Each (The Social Framework)

4. **Uranus, Neptune, and Pluto:** 0.5 Points Each (The Generational Backdrop)

Calculation Steps:

- List every planet and the sign it occupies.
- Categorize those signs by element (e.g., Aries = Fire, Taurus = Earth).
- Add up the points for each element.

The Phenomenon of the "Empty Element"

It is rare to be perfectly balanced. Most people discover they are "deficient" in one element. In psychological astrology, a missing element acts as a "vacuum"—it is something you constantly feel you are lacking, so you often spend your whole life trying to compensate for it.

- **Missing Fire:** You may feel you lack "drive," so you overcompensate by becoming hyper-disciplined or surrounding yourself with high-energy people.
- **Missing Earth:** You may feel "unrooted," so you become obsessed with spreadsheets, organization, and minimalism to try and force a sense of stability.
- **Missing Air:** You may feel you aren't "smart enough," so you become a perpetual student, collecting degrees and books to prove your intellectual worth.
- **Missing Water:** You may feel "numb," so you seek out intense, dramatic relationships or art to force yourself to feel the depth you think you are missing.

Elemental Compatibility in Relationships and Work

Understanding elements is the fastest way to improve your relationships. Conflict often arises not from bad intentions, but from "Elemental Mismatch."

- **Fire/Air:** A productive mix. Air fans the flames of Fire's ideas.
- **Earth/Water:** A nurturing mix. Water softens Earth, and Earth gives Water a container.

- **Fire/Water:** Volatile. Water can douse Fire's enthusiasm; Fire can make Water feel "boiled" or overwhelmed.

- **Air/Earth:** Productive but dry. Air provides the plan, and Earth builds it, but there may be a lack of passion or emotional warmth.

Mini-Workbook: Your Elemental Audit

Using the point system above, tally your scores:

- **Total Fire Score:** ____
- **Total Earth Score:** _______________________________________
- **Total Air Score:** ____
- **Total Water Score:** _______________________________________

1. **The Dominant Force:** Which element has the highest score? Does this match your "default" energy? (e.g., Do you always feel "fired up" or "grounded"?)

   ____

   ____

   ____

2. **The Scarcity Point:** Which element is your lowest? How have you seen yourself try to "fake" or "compensate" for this energy in your life?

   ____

   ____

   ____

3. **The Environmental Check:** If you are "High Water" but work in a "High Air" (logical, cold, corporate) environment, how can you introduce more of your natural element into your workspace to avoid burnout?

   ____

   ____

   ____

Chapter 2: Modalities and Movement

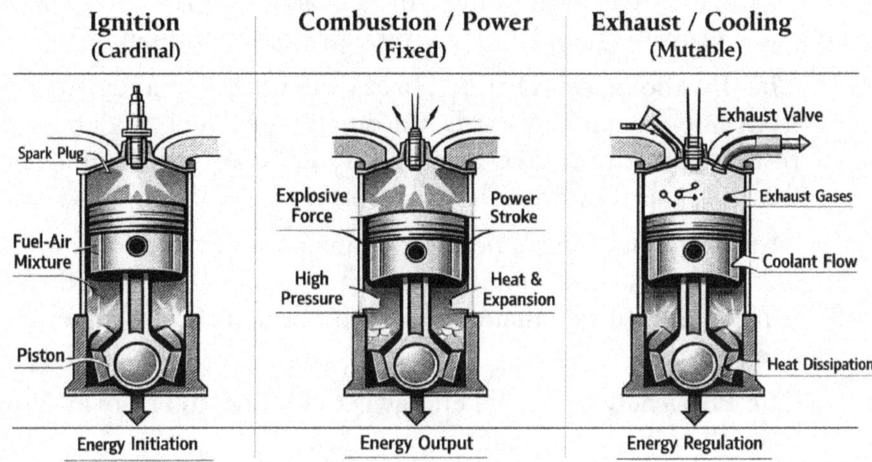

Cardinal, Fixed, and Mutable: Your Approach to Change

If the elements (Fire, Earth, Air, and Water) represent the **substance** of your personality, the Modalities represent its **motion.** In physics, matter exists in different states, solid, liquid, or gas, but it also moves in different ways: acceleration, steady velocity, or shifting direction. In astrology, the three modalities (also known as "Qualities") describe how you use your energy to interact with time and environmental pressure.

Every zodiac sign is a combination of an element and a modality. No two signs share the same combination. This is the "DNA" of the zodiac. For example, Aries is Fire (element) and Cardinal (modality). Leo is Fire and Fixed. Sagittarius is Fire and Mutable. While they all share the "Fire" fuel, they use that fuel in completely different ways. Understanding your dominant modality explains why you might be a great "starter" but a poor "finisher," or why you might be the "anchor" that holds a team together during a crisis.

The Cardinal Modality: The Power of Initiation

Signs: Aries, Cancer, Libra, Capricorn

Cardinal energy corresponds to the beginning of the four seasons: the Spring Equinox, the Summer Solstice, the Autumn Equinox, and the Winter Solstice. Astronomically, these are points of "turning." Consequently, Cardinal people are the **pioneers** of the human race.

- **The Psychological Drive:** This is centrifugal energy; it moves from the center outward. Cardinal types feel a deep, often restless, need to "make an impact." They are not content to let things stay as they are. They are driven by the "New."

- **The Temperament:** These individuals are "crisis-movers." They are at their best when a new project is launching, a new direction is needed, or a stalemate needs to be broken. They value impact and progress.

- **The Physicality:** Cardinal energy is often high-intensity and short-burst. It is the sprinter of the zodiac.

- **The Shadow:** The "Restless Spirit." Cardinal types can become addicted to the rush of starting. Once the "newness" wears off and the hard work of maintenance begins, they may lose interest and abandon the project for a fresh thrill. This can lead to a trail of half-finished ideas and exhausted partners.

The Fixed Modality: The Power of Persistence

Signs: Taurus, Leo, Scorpio, Aquarius

Fixed signs occur in the middle of the seasons, when the weather is at its most stable and established. This is the "heart" of the season. Fixed people are the **sustainers** and the **architects** of the human race.

- **The Psychological Drive:** This is centripetal energy; it moves toward the center and holds firm. Fixed types are driven by the need for depth, mastery, and endurance. They do not want to start ten things; they want to perfect one thing.

- **The Temperament:** These are the "anchors." Once they decide on a path, they are nearly impossible to move. They value loyalty, reliability, and structural integrity. They provide the "follow-through" that the Cardinal types lack.

- **The Physicality:** Fixed energy is slow-burn. It is the marathon runner of the zodiac. It can endure immense pressure without cracking.

- **The Shadow:** "The Rigidity." The shadow of Fixed energy is stubbornness. Because they value stability so highly, they find change fundamentally threatening. They may stay in a toxic job or a dead relationship for years because the act of "pivoting" feels like a personal failure.

The Mutable Modality: The Power of Adaptation

Signs: Gemini, Virgo, Sagittarius, Pisces

Mutable signs occur at the end of the seasons, when one phase of life is dissolving into the next. The air is changing; the light is shifting. Mutable people are the **translators** and **editors** of the human race.

- **The Psychological Drive:** This is spiral energy: it moves in many directions at once. Mutable energy is about flexibility, transition, and the distribution of information.

- **The Temperament:** These are the "adapters." They are at their best when things are in flux and everyone else is panicking. They can see multiple perspectives and are quick to pivot when a plan fails. They value wisdom, variety, and change.

- **The Physicality:** Mutable energy is fluctuating. It is the dancer of the zodiac. It is agile and light, capable of moving through tight spaces that would trap a Fixed or Cardinal type.

- **The Shadow:** "The Dissipation." Mutable types can struggle with a lack of core identity. Because they are so good at mirroring their surroundings, they may feel "scattered" or find it difficult to stand their ground when a decision is required.

The Modality Mix:
Finding Your Operational Style

In professional astrology, we look at the "weight" of the modalities in your chart to determine your **Operational Style.** This is often more important than your sign for determining your career path.

Balance	The Operational Result
High Cardinal / Low Fixed	The Visionary. You start businesses easily but need to hire "Fixed" people to manage the day-to-day operations or you will burn out.
High Fixed / Low Mutable	The Specialist. You are a master of your craft, but you may be rendered obsolete if you don't learn to adapt to new technologies or trends.
High Mutable / Low Cardinal	The Consultant. You are brilliant at fixing other people's problems and adapting to change, but you may wait for "permission" before starting your own projects.

Historical and Archetypal Roles

Throughout history, these modalities formed the backbone of community survival.

- **Cardinal types** were the scouts and explorers who found new land and resources.

- **Fixed types** were the builders and farmers who cleared the land, built the walls, and ensured the community survived the winter.

- **Mutable types** were the storytellers, teachers, and merchants who traveled between villages, sharing knowledge and ensuring the culture evolved.

If you are a Fixed person trying to be a "scout," you will feel slow and incompetent. If you are a Cardinal person trying to be a "builder," you will feel bored and trapped. **Happiness is the result of aligning your work with your natural modality.**

Mini-Workbook: Modality Tally

Refer back to your Planetary Inventory from Book 1 and assign points:

(Sun/Moon/AC = 3 pts | Mercury/Venus/Mars = 2 pts | Jupiter/Saturn = 1 pt)

- **Cardinal Score:** _____________ (Aries, Cancer, Libra, Capricorn)
- **Fixed Score:** _____________ (Taurus, Leo, Scorpio, Aquarius)
- **Mutable Score:** _________ (Gemini, Virgo, Sagittarius, Pisces)

1. **The Finisher vs. The Starter:** Looking at your scores, are you more likely to jump into something new or struggle to let go of something old?

   ____

   ____

   ____

2. **The Pivot Test:** Recall the last major change in your life (a move, a job change, a breakup). Did you initiate it (Cardinal), resist it (Fixed), or just flow with it (Mutable)? How does this match your scores?

   ____

   ____

   ____

3. **Growth Strategy:** If you are "Low Fixed," what is one small habit you can commit to for 30 days to build your persistence "muscle"?

   ____

   ____

   ____

Chapter 3: The Lunar Nodes

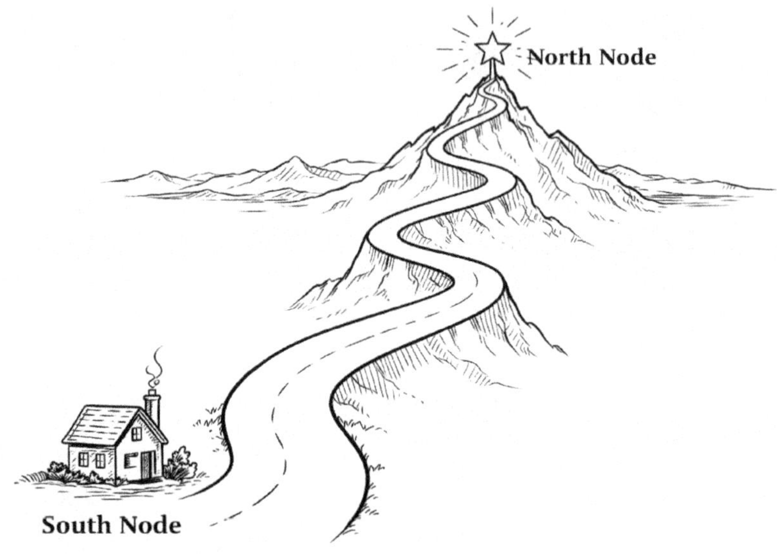

Identifying Past Habits and Future Growth Points

While the planets represent the different parts of your psyche, the Lunar Nodes, known as the **North Node** and the **South Node**, represent your trajectory. They are not physical objects, but the points where the orbit of the Moon crosses the ecliptic (the path of the Sun). In the history of astrology, these have been called the "Dragon's Head" (Rahu) and the "Dragon's Tail" (Ketu). Together, they form the **Nodal Axis**, a line of destiny that describes where you are coming from and where you are meant to go.

Understanding your Nodes is often the most profound part of a chart reading because it explains your "default settings" versus your "soul's calling." The South Node represents what is comfortable, practiced, and easy, while the North Node represents the "uncharted territory" that feels intimidating but offers the greatest reward.

The South Node: The Path of Least Resistance

The South Node represents your "factory settings." Whether you believe in past lives or genetic memory, the South Node describes the traits and behaviors that you were born knowing how to do.

- **The Experience:** It feels like a safe harbor. It is where you go when you are tired or stressed. For example, if your South Node is in the 10th House of Career, you may be naturally excellent at professional life and public achievement.

- **The Trap:** Because the South Node is so easy, we can become "stuck" there. Staying entirely in your South Node is like staying in kindergarten because you are the smartest kid in the room. There is no growth, and eventually, life begins to feel stagnant or hollow. The South Node is a "gift" you are meant to use as a foundation, not a place to live permanently.

The North Node: The North Star of the Soul

The North Node is always exactly 180 degrees opposite the South Node. It represents the qualities you need to develop in this lifetime to feel truly fulfilled.

- **The Experience:** It often feels awkward, scary, or "not like me." Using our previous example, if your South Node is in the 10th House (Public Success), your North Node will be in the 4th House (Home/Privacy). Your growth point in this life is not to work harder, but to learn how to nurture your inner world and family life.

- **The Reward:** When you lean into your North Node, doors seem to open. Even though it feels difficult, it provides a sense of deep, existential satisfaction that the South Node can no longer provide.

The 18-Year Cycle: The Nodal Return

The Nodes take approximately 18.6 years to move through the entire zodiac. This means that every 18–19 years (at ages 18, 37, 56, and 74), you experience a **Nodal Return.** These are often "pivotal years" where you are forced to confront whether you are living in your South Node comfort zone or moving toward your North Node purpose.

During a Nodal Return, life often "corrects" your course. If you have been hiding in your South Node, you may experience a crisis that pushes you toward your North Node. If you are already moving toward your growth point, these years often bring major breakthroughs and a sense of "alignment" with your destiny.

Interpreting the Axis: A Guide to the Signs

To understand your specific "Roadmap," look at the sign and house placement of your North Node. The South Node is automatically the opposite.

North Node Placement	The Past Habit (South Node)	The Future Growth (North Node)
Aries / 1st House	Over-compromising; losing self in others.	Developing independence and self-assertion.
Taurus / 2nd House	Living for the "crisis"; reliance on others.	Building self-worth and material stability.
Gemini / 3rd House	Over-intellectualizing; dogmatic beliefs.	Curiosity, local connection, and listening.
Cancer / 4th House	Obsession with public status and control.	Emotional vulnerability and domestic peace.
Leo / 5th House	Hiding in the group; being "cool/detached."	Personal creativity and heart-centered risk.
Virgo / 6th House	Escapism; lack of boundaries; "victim" mindset.	Routine, practical service, and discernment.
Libra / 7th House	Aggressive "me-first" attitude; selfishness.	Partnership, diplomacy, and cooperation.

North Node Placement	The Past Habit (South Node)	The Future Growth (North Node)
Scorpio / 8th House	Clinging to safety; fear of deep change.	Psychological depth and shared intimacy.
Sagittarius / 9th House	Getting lost in small details/gossip.	Seeking the "Big Picture" and higher truth.
Capricorn / 10th House	Emotional over-dependence; "childlike" fear.	Taking authority and professional responsibility.
Aquarius / 11th House	Need for constant attention and ego-praise.	Serving the collective and the "greater good."
Pisces / 12th House	Workaholism; obsession with "perfection."	Surrender, spirituality, and compassion.

The Integration: Walking the Tightrope

A common mistake is thinking you must "abandon" your South Node. This is impossible and unwise. Your South Node is your **talent.** Your North Node is your **direction.** The goal is to use your South Node talents to achieve your North Node goals. If you have a South Node in Gemini (great communication), use that gift to teach the higher truths of your Sagittarius North Node.

Synthesis is the key. You are not choosing one side of the line over the other; you are learning how to walk the line between the person you were and the person you are becoming.

Mini-Workbook: The Nodal Compass

Refer to your **Planetary Inventory** or chart to find your North Node (☊).

- **North Node Sign:** ______________________________________
- **North Node House:** ____________________________________
- **South Node Sign:** ____________ (Opposite your North Node)

1. **The Safety Blanket:** Look at the description of your South Node above. In what area of your life do you "play it safe"? When you are stressed, do you find yourself reverting to these habits?

____

____

____

2. **The Call to Adventure:** Look at your North Node. What is one activity or trait related to this sign that feels "scary but exciting" to you? (e.g., If North Node is in Leo, it might be public speaking or performing).

____

____

____

3. **The Course Correction:** Think back to a "Nodal Return" year (roughly age 18 or 37). Did you experience a major change that forced you to leave a comfort zone? Describe that shift.

____

____

____

Chapter 4: Chiron and the Wounded Healer

Addressing Recurring Personal Challenges

In 1977, astronomers discovered a small, icy body orbiting between Saturn and Uranus. Named **Chiron**, it was classified as a "Centaur": a celestial object that behaves like both an asteroid and a comet. In the language of astrology, Chiron's placement between the "limitations" of Saturn and the "rebellion" of Uranus is deeply symbolic. It represents the bridge between our physical pain and our spiritual awakening.

In Greek mythology, Chiron was a centaur who was an expert in medicine, music, and prophecy. Despite being a master healer for others, he suffered from a chronic, incurable wound. This myth provides the core archetype for the planetoid: **The Wounded Healer.** In your birth chart, Chiron marks the place where you feel "broken," inadequate, or uniquely sensitive. However, this very wound is the key to your greatest wisdom.

The Nature of the Chironic Wound

Unlike the challenges of Mars (which we solve through action) or Saturn (which we solve through discipline), the Chironic wound is often something that cannot be fully "fixed." It is a recurring theme of inadequacy.

- **The Experience:** It feels like a "tender spot" in your psyche. For example, if Chiron is in your 3rd House of Communication, you may have grown up feeling unintelligent or struggled with speech, despite being highly capable.

- **The Gift:** Because you have suffered in this area, you develop an extraordinary level of empathy and expertise regarding that specific pain. The person with Chiron in the 3rd House often becomes a gifted writer or teacher because they understand the mechanics of communication better than those for whom it comes easily.

Chiron Through the Houses: Where You Heal

To find your "Wounded Healer" energy, look at the house where the Chiron symbol ($\text{\char"26B7}$) is located in your chart.

House Placement	The Core Wound	The Healing Gift
1st House	Feeling invisible or "wrong" for existing.	Helping others claim their identity.
2nd House	Feeling "not enough" or financially unstable.	Teaching the true meaning of self-worth.
3rd House	Feeling misunderstood or intellectually "lesser."	Mastery of words and original thinking.
4th House	Feeling unrooted or "unwanted" in the family.	Creating emotional safety for others.
5th House	Feeling "un-creative" or unable to play.	Sparking the creative fire in others.

House Placement	The Core Wound	The Healing Gift
6th House	Constant struggle with health or "perfection."	Giftedness in alternative health and service.
7th House	Feeling "unlovable" or failed by partners.	Deep wisdom in counseling and diplomacy.
8th House	Fear of intimacy, loss, or deep change.	Helping others through crisis and grief.
9th House	Loss of faith or feeling "directionless."	Acting as a guide or spiritual philosopher.
10th House	Feeling like a "fraud" in your career.	Leading others with humility and integrity.
11th House	Feeling like an outcast from the "tribe."	Building communities for the misunderstood.
12th House	Feeling overwhelmed by universal suffering.	Profound spiritual empathy and healing.

The Chiron Return: The 50-Year Milestone

Chiron takes approximately 50 years to orbit the Sun. This makes the **Chiron Return** (occurring around age 49–51) one of the most significant transition points in a human life.

Before this age, we often try to "fix" or hide our Chironic wound. We feel shame about our inadequacies. However, during the Chiron Return, we are invited to stop trying to be "perfect" and instead accept the wound as a part of our mastery. This is often the time when people move from being "students of life" to being "mentors for others." It is the moment when the "Wounded Healer" finally accepts their medicine.

Integration: Turning Lead into Gold

The secret to working with Chiron is to stop viewing the pain as an obstacle and start seeing it as an **altar.** Your greatest struggle is the very thing that connects you to the rest of humanity.

If you have Chiron in the 2nd House (Money/Security), you may always feel a bit anxious about finances, no matter how much you have. Instead of trying to delete that anxiety, use it to develop a superior understanding of value. Your "wound" is the lens through which you see the world most clearly.

Mini-Workbook: The Healer's Inquiry

Refer to your **Planetary Inventory** or chart to find Chiron ($\text{\char"26B7}$).

- **Chiron House:** ____

- **Chiron Sign:** ____

1. **The Recurring Insecurity:** Looking at the house placement above, what is one area of life where you always feel "behind" or "not quite good enough," despite evidence to the contrary?

   ____

   ____

   ____

2. **The Accidental Expertise:** Think of a time you helped someone else through a problem. Did that problem relate to your Chiron house? (e.g., helping a friend through a breakup when you feel "bad" at relationships).

   ____

   ____

   ____

3. **The Acceptance Shift:** How would your life change if you stopped trying to "cure" this insecurity and instead treated it as a "sensitive teacher"?

   ____

   ____

   ____

Chapter 5: Signature Signs

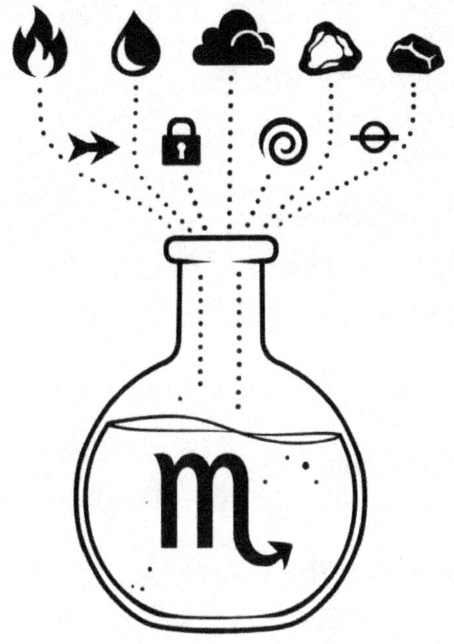

How to Find the Dominant Energy of Your Chart

Up to this point, you have analyzed your chart through various lenses: the "Big Three" pillars, the elemental "fuel," and the modal "rhythm." However, a central question remains: *If my Sun is in one sign, but my elements and modalities point to another, which one is the "true" leader of my personality?* In professional astrology, we solve this by calculating your **Signature Sign.**

The Signature Sign is a technical calculation that identifies the single zodiac sign that best summarizes the mathematical "weight" of your entire chart. It is common to discover that your Signature Sign is different from your Sun sign. For example, you might be a Sun in Libra, but your Signature Sign is Scorpio. This explains why you might feel more intense, private, and investigative than the typical "harmonious" Libra description suggest.

The Mathematical Logic of the Signature

The Signature Sign is not based on "feelings" or "intuition"; it is based on the combination of your **Dominant Element** and your **Dominant Modality.** As we explored in previous chapters, every zodiac sign is a unique pairing of these two qualities.

- Fire + Cardinal = Aries
- Fire + Fixed = Leo
- Fire + Mutable = Sagittarius
- Earth + Cardinal = Capricorn
- Earth + Fixed = Taurus
- Earth + Mutable = Virgo
- Air + Cardinal = Libra
- Air + Fixed = Aquarius
- Air + Mutable = Gemini
- Water + Cardinal = Cancer
- Water + Fixed = Scorpio
- Water + Mutable = Pisces

By identifying which element and which modality have the most "points" in your chart (using the weighting system from Chapter 1 and 2), you find the intersection point. That intersection is your **Signature Sign.**

The Psychological "Dominant Function"

In Jungian psychology, every individual has a "Dominant Function": the primary way they orient themselves to the world. For some, it is Thinking; for others, it is Feeling, Sensation, or Intuition. Your Signature Sign is the astrological equivalent of this function. It represents your "default setting."

When your Sun sign and your Signature Sign are different, you possess a "Dual Identity." Your Sun sign represents your **goal,** who you are learning to become, while your Signature Sign represents your **process,** how you naturally act. Understanding this distinction can end years of self-judgment. If your Sun is in an outgoing sign like Aries, but your Signature is an introverted sign like Pisces, you might have felt "guilty" for needing so much solitude. Once you realize Pisces is your Signature, you can accept that your path to "Aries leadership" must be fueled by "Piscean empathy."

The "Unresolved" Signature: When the Math is a Tie

Sometimes, the calculation results in a tie. You might have equal points in Fire and Water, or equal points in Cardinal and Fixed. In these cases, you are said to have an **Unresolved Signature.**

This indicates a "Complex" personality type. You are not meant to be a single, streamlined energy; you are meant to be a bridge between two different modes of being. An unresolved signature often leads to a person who is highly versatile but may struggle with internal "flickering," where they move between two different ways of acting depending on their environment.

The Impact of the Signature on Career and Relationships

While the Sun sign tells us *what* you want to do, the Signature Sign tells us *how* you will do it.

- **In Career:** A person with a **Fixed/Earth (Taurus)** signature will thrive in long-term projects that require physical endurance, regardless of their Sun sign.

- **In Relationships:** A person with a **Mutable/Air (Gemini)** signature will always need intellectual variety and "breathing room" in a partnership, even if their Sun sign is a "clinging" sign like Cancer.

By identifying your Signature, you can stop trying to force yourself into roles that don't match your energetic "wiring." You gain the authority to say, *"I know my Sun sign is supposed to be social, but my Signature is Fixed and Private, and I need to honor that."*

Mini-Workbook: Calculating Your Signature

Refer back to your tallies in Chapter 1 (Elements) and Chapter 2 (Modalities).

1. **Your Dominant Element:**_______________________________
   (The one with the highest score)

2. **Your Dominant Modality:** ____________________________
   (The one with the highest score)

3. **The Signature Intersection:** Combine them using the list above.

   My Signature Sign is: ____________________________

The Comparison:

- Is your Signature Sign the same as your Sun sign? _________
- If they are different, look up the "Short Description" for your Signature Sign. Does this "process" describe your daily habits better than your Sun sign does?

____

____

____

____

Conclusion: Embracing the Contradictions within Your Personality

The Myth of the Monolith

We are raised in a culture that demands consistency. We are told that to be a "strong" person, we must be one thing: reliable, predictable, and easily categorized. In the workplace, we are encouraged to "brand" ourselves; in relationships, we are expected to play a stable, unchanging role. However, the deeper you journey into your birth chart, the more you realize that the human psyche is not a monolith. It is a vibrant, often clashing ecosystem. This final section of **Book 2** is dedicated to the most difficult part of the astrological journey: moving from the clinical analysis of your separate "parts" to the psychological acceptance of your **Integrated Self.**

As you look back over the chapters of this book, you might feel a sense of internal friction. Perhaps you have discovered that while your **Sun sign** (your core vitality) wants to be seen and celebrated in the public sphere, your **Signature Sign** (your operational default) is fundamentally introverted and cautious. Or perhaps your **North Node** is calling you toward spiritual surrender while your **Chiron** wound keeps you hyper-vigilant about physical security. In traditional logic, these are "contradictions." In the language of the soul, they are **Dialectics.**

The Dialectics of the Self

In philosophy, a dialectic is a discourse between two seemingly opposing points of view that eventually leads to a higher truth. Your birth chart is a lifelong dialectic.

Consider the person with an **Air-dominant temperament** but a **Fixed modality.** Air is an element that naturally wants to circulate, move, and connect. However, the Fixed modality wants to stay put, concentrate, and endure. This person might feel like a "circulating anchor." They may have a brilliant, fast-moving mind, but they find it agonizingly difficult to change their physical circumstances or "let go" of an idea once it has taken root.

When we do not understand our chart, we judge this as a flaw. We call ourselves "stuck" or "inconsistent." But when we embrace the synthesis, we see the gift: this is the person who can take a complex, shifting idea (Air) and have the iron-willed persistence (Fixed) to see it through to completion over a decade. The "contradiction" is actually their **Competitive Advantage.**

Archetypal Friction: Why Harmony is Overrated

There is a common misconception that a "good" birth chart is one where all the planets are in harmonious aspects (trines and sextiles). While these "blue lines" represent ease and talent, a chart filled only with harmony often lacks the "engine" required for significant personal growth.

It is the **Square** and the **Opposition**, the red lines of friction, that force us to evolve. If your identity (Sun) is square your sense of duty (Saturn), you will spend your life feeling a tension between who you want to be and what you feel you "must" do. This friction is the heat that forges the steel of your character. As the psychologist James Hillman often noted, the "afflictions" of our nature are often the very things that make us unique. Without the "wound" of Chiron or the "pull" of the Nodes, we would be perfectly balanced, perfectly boring, and perfectly stagnant.

The Integration: From "Either/Or" to "Both/And"

The culmination of "Discovering Your Cosmic Identity" is the transition from **Either/Or** thinking to **Both/And** thinking.

- *I am not either a leader (Sun in Leo) or a servant (Signature in Virgo); I am a leader who leads through meticulous service.*

- *I am not either wounded (Chiron in the 4th) or successful (North Node in the 10th); I am a person whose public authority is rooted in their private healing.*

Book 2 has provided you with the technical map. You now know your fuel (Elements), your rhythm (Modalities), and your path (Nodes). But a map is not the journey. The journey is the act of "Living the Chart": the moment-to-moment decision to stop apologizing for your complexity and start utilizing it as a tool for self-mastery.

The Road Ahead: Book 3

You have now established the structural foundations **(Book 1)** and the energetic identity **(Book 2)**. You are no longer looking at your chart as a stranger. You are seeing a reflection that, while complex and perhaps a bit messy, is authentically yours.

In the upcoming **Book 3: The Twelve Great Paths**, we will take this identity and move it through the twelve archetypal stories of the human experience. We will dive deep into the specific psychology of the signs, Aries through Pisces, exploring their myths, their shadows, and their highest potentials. You will learn how to inhabit these signs not as "labels," but as living energies that you can call upon as you navigate your life.

Synthesis Exercise: The Integration Statement

To close this book, write a statement that honors your most significant internal contradiction.

"While my [Element/Modality] nature makes me feel [Default Trait], my [Node/Chiron] path is calling me to [Growth Goal]. I choose to use my [Default Trait] to help me achieve [Growth Goal]."

Example: "While my Fixed/Earth signature makes me feel a need for total control, my North Node in Pisces is calling me to learn surrender. I choose to use my grounded stability to create a safe space where I can finally learn to let go."

Reflection Questions: Integrating Your Cosmic Identity

Layer 1: The Elemental Fuel

1. **Energy Patterns:** Look at your highest elemental score. How does this "fuel" manifest in your daily life? For example, if you are high in Fire, do you find yourself rushing into projects? If high in Earth, do you feel a physical need for structure and touch?

    ____

    ____

    ____

2. **The Vacuum:** Looking at your lowest elemental score, identify a time you felt "out of your depth" in a situation that required that specific energy. How did you handle it? Did you try to "fake" the energy, or did you seek help from someone who possesses it naturally?

    ____

    ____

    ____

Layer 2: The Modal engine

3. **The Starting Line:** Are you a Cardinal "Starter," a Fixed "Sustainer," or a Mutable "Adapter"? Think of a major project you abandoned. Was it because the "newness" wore off (Cardinal), it became too rigid (Fixed), or you got distracted by a new perspective (Mutable)?

    ____

    ____

    ____

    ____

4. **Reaction to Stress:** When a sudden change is forced upon you, what is your immediate visceral reaction? Do you immediately try to lead the change, resist it to maintain the status quo, or shift your shape to fit the new reality?

    ____

    ____

    ____

    ____

Layer 3: The Soul's Trajectory

5. **The South Node Trap:** What is one "talent" or habit that comes so easily to you that you often use it as a hiding place? How can you tell when you are leaning too heavily on this "past" energy at the expense of your growth?

    ____

    ____

    ____

    ____

6. **The North Node Calling:** Think of a person you admire. Do they embody the traits of your North Node sign? Often, we are attracted to people who represent the evolutionary path we are meant to walk.

    ____

    ____

    ____

Layer 4: The Healer's Journey

7. **The Insecurity Source:** Look at your Chiron house placement. If you were to give a speech to a group of people suffering from that specific "wound," what is the most important piece of wisdom you could offer them? (Remember: Your wound is where your greatest expertise lies).

____

____

____

Layer 5: The Signature Synthesis

8. **The Internal Dialogue:** If your Sun Sign and your Signature Sign were two different people sitting at a table together, what would they be arguing about? What would they eventually agree on?

____

____

____

Final Self-Assessment:
The Three Pillars of Identity

Pillar	My Finding	What this means for my daily life
Temperament	(Dominant Element)	
Operational Mode	(Dominant Modality)	
Evolutionary Goal	(North Node Sign/House)	

Workbook Section 2:
The Identity Inventory

Part 1: The Elemental & Modal Scoring Sheet

To find your **Signature Sign**, you must look at the distribution of your planets. Use your birth chart to fill in the tallies below.

> **Scoring Rule:** Assign 1 point for each planet (Sun through Pluto). Assign 2 points for your **Ascendant** and **Midheaven**, as these are high-impact mathematical points.

Table A: The Elemental Tally

Element	Planets/Points	Total Score
Fire (Ari, Leo, Sag)		
Earth (Tau, Vir, Cap)		
Air (Gem, Lib, Aqu)		
Water (Can, Sco, Pis)		

Table B: The Modal Tally

Modality	Planets/Points	Total Score
Cardinal (Ari, Can, Lib, Cap)		
Fixed (Tau, Leo, Sco, Aqu)		
Mutable (Gem, Vir, Sag, Pis)		

Part 2: Defining Your Signature Sign

Your **Signature Sign** is the zodiac sign that represents the *flavor* of your combined scores, even if you have no planets in that actual sign.

1. **Dominant Element:** ____
   (The fuel you run on)

2. **Dominant Modality:** ____
   (The way you move)

3. **Your Signature Sign:** ____
   (Example: Fire + Mutable = Sagittarius Signature)

Reflective Prompt: Does your Signature Sign feel more like "the real you" than your Sun Sign? Why or why not?

____

____

____

____

Part 3: The Evolutionary Compass (Nodes & Chiron)

This section maps your soul's trajectory: where you are coming from and where you are headed.

1. The Comfort Zone (South Node)

- **Sign & House:** ____

- **The Talent:** What comes so naturally to you that you often do it without thinking?

____

____

____

- **The Trap:** How does this talent keep you from trying new, difficult things?

____

____

____

2. The Growing Edge (North Node)

- **Sign & House:** ____

- **The Challenge:** What set of traits feels "awkward" or "unnatural" to you, yet highly rewarding when you practice them?

  ____

  ____

3. The Master Healer (Chiron)

- **House Placement:** ____

- **The Wound:** In which area of life (Money, Communication, Family, etc.) do you feel a recurring sense of "not being enough"?

  ____

  ____

- **The Medicine:** How has struggling with this wound made you more compassionate or knowledgeable than someone who has never faced it?

  ____

  ____

Part 4: Identity Synthesis Statement

Fill in the blanks to create a cohesive summary of your Book 2 findings. This statement serves as the foundation for the "Purpose Planning" we will do in Book 3.

> "Though my Sun is in **[Sun Sign]**, my internal engine runs on the energy of **[Signature Sign]**. I am currently evolving away from the habit of **[South Node Trait]** and toward the courage of **[North Node Trait]**. My greatest challenge lies in my **[Chiron House]**, but through this struggle, I am developing the unique gift of **[Wisdom/Strength]**."

BOOK THREE
Use the Zodiac to Navigate Life with Purpose

Introduction:
Applying Astrological Timing to Decision-Making and Career

The Architecture of Time

The most common misconception about astrology is that it is a system of "fixed fate." People often ask, *"What is going to happen to me?"* as if they are passive observers of their own lives, waiting for the stars to dictate their joy or their sorrow. However, authoritative astrology views time not as a straight line of inevitable events, but as a series of **recurring, concentric cycles.**

Every planet in our solar system has a rhythm, a "metabolism" of movement. The Moon changes signs every two days, influencing our fleeting moods; Saturn takes twenty-nine years to circle the zodiac, influencing the structural foundations of our character. When these moving planets (known in astrology as **Transits**) interact with the stationary planets in your birth chart, they create "windows of opportunity." Understanding this timing is the difference between swimming against a powerful tide and surfing a wave at its peak. In **Book 3**, we move from the self-analysis of "Who am I?" to the strategic execution of **"When is the right time?"**

The Historical Shift: From Omen to Strategy

In the ancient world, from the ziggurats of Babylon to the courts of the Renaissance, astrology was primarily a tool for "Electional" timing—the art of choosing the exact moment to crown a king, launch a naval fleet, or sign a peace treaty. In those eras, time was seen as a resource as tangible as gold or grain.

Today, we apply these same principles to modern navigation. We are no longer launching fleets, but we are launching startups, pivoting careers, and entering long-term partnerships. By aligning these actions with planetary cycles, we are effectively "seeding" our intentions in fertile soil.

- **Career Pivots:** We use the **Midheaven (MC)** and its transits to identify not just what you are good at, but when the public and the marketplace are most receptive to your unique skill set.

- **Relationship Dynamics:** Through **Synastry**, we analyze how your energetic field interacts with another person's, identifying seasons of harmony and seasons where "work" is required to bridge the gap.

- **Personal Maturity:** We prepare for the major "thresholds" of life, such as the **Saturn Return**, which acts as a cosmic performance review, stripping away what is obsolete to make room for what is essential.

The Concept of "Kairos" vs. "Chronos"

The Greeks utilized two distinct words for time, a distinction that is central to the work we will do in **Book 3**. *Chronos* is chronological, quantitative time—the relentless, sequential ticking of the clock that measures our age and our deadlines. *Kairos*, however, is qualitative time; it refers to the "opportune moment," the moment where the internal state of a person meets the external readiness of the world.

Astrology is the study of *Kairos*. It teaches us that time is not flat; it has texture. There are "Saturnian" years designed for quiet, internal consolidation and the building of discipline. There are "Jupiterian" years designed for radical external expansion and risk-taking. If you try to force a massive career expansion during a year meant for deep internal healing, you will likely experience burnout and frustration. Conversely, if you recognize a favorable transit to your Midheaven, you can move with the confidence that the universe is providing the "wind" at your back.

The Living, Evolving Chart

While **Book 1** and **Book 2** focused on your "Natal" chart, the map of your birth, **Book 3** introduces the concept of the **Progressed Chart**. If the birth chart is the original seed, the progressed chart is the growing tree.

As we age, our needs, interests, and temperaments shift. A person born with a quiet, introverted Moon may find that, through progression, their emotional needs become more expressive and outgoing as they reach their thirties. This explains the phenomenon of "second acts" in life: why a lifelong accountant might suddenly find their voice as an artist or why a wanderer might suddenly crave a permanent home. Progressions show us how our soul is maturing from the inside out, ensuring that we never remain static.

By the end of this book, you will no longer view your life as a series of random, disconnected occurrences. You will see it as a structured, purposeful journey. You will have the technical tools to plan your next twelve months with the precision of a celestial navigator, ensuring that your most important life decisions are made in perfect sync with the natural, rhythmic cycles of the cosmos.

Mini-Workbook: Your Relationship with Timing

1. **The "Right" Moment:** Think of a time in your life when everything seemed to "click" effortlessly (a job offer, meeting a significant partner, a sudden creative breakthrough). Write down the approximate date. We will revisit this in Chapter 2 to see which transits were active.

    ____

    ____

    ____

2. **The "Upstairs" Struggle:** Recall a season when you worked incredibly hard but felt like you were hitting a brick wall at every turn. Did this happen during a specific age threshold? (e.g., age 28-30 or age 42-44).

    ____

    ____

    ____

3. **Vocational Intent:** If you could strategically time one major professional move in the next year, what would it be? (Examples: asking for a raise, launching a project, or leaving a current role). We will apply the "Midheaven" lens to this goal in Chapter 4.

Chapter 1: Saturn Returns and Maturity

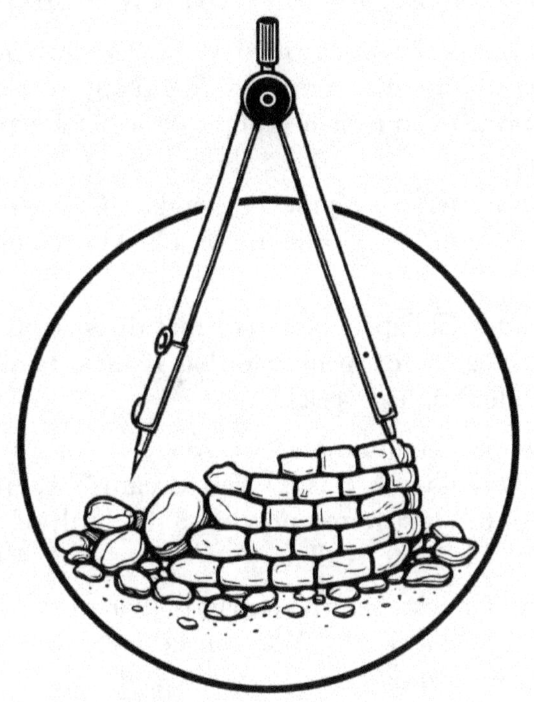

The Great Teacher: Facing the Threshold at Ages 29, 58, and 87

In the hierarchy of the solar system, Saturn is the last planet visible to the naked human eye. For millennia, this made Saturn the "Lord of the Boundaries." It represented the limit of what we could see, touch, and control. In your birth chart, Saturn is the symbol of structure, discipline, responsibility, and, most importantly, time.

The **Saturn Return** is an astronomical event that occurs when the planet Saturn completes its full orbit around the Sun and returns to the exact degree and sign it occupied at the moment of your birth. This journey takes approximately 29.5 years. Because Saturn moves so slowly, its "return" isn't a single day, but a period of roughly two to three years where the universe holds up a mirror to your life and asks: *"Is the foundation you have built strong enough to support the person you are becoming?"*

The First Return (Ages 27–30): The End of Youth

The first Saturn Return is often described as the "Cosmic Bar Mitzvah" or the true entry into adulthood. Before age 29, many of our choices are reactions to our upbringing, our peer groups, or societal expectations. We are "practicing" at life.

When Saturn returns, the "practice" ends. This period is often characterized by a sense of heavy pressure or a "ticking clock" feeling. You may experience:

- **The Structural Collapse:** A career that doesn't fit, a relationship that lacks integrity, or a lifestyle that is unsustainable will often crumble under Saturn's weight.

- **The Defining Commitment:** Conversely, for those who have done the internal work, this is when "dreams" become "careers." It is the age of the first home purchase, the birth of a child, or the definitive "yes" to a life's calling.

- **The Reality Check:** Saturn demands that we trade our infinite potential for actual results. You can no longer be "anything"; you must finally be *something*.

The Second Return (Ages 56–60): The Mastery of Purpose

If the first return is about becoming an adult, the second return is about becoming an **Elder**. This is the transition from the "doing" phase of life to the "mentoring" phase.

At age 58, Saturn asks: *"What have you done with the authority you've gained?"* This return often coincides with a "Third Act" career shift or a deep reassessment of one's legacy. It is a time when the ego's drive for external validation begins to fade, replaced by a desire for meaningful contribution. For many, this is the most liberating Saturn Return, as the pressure to "prove oneself" to the world is finally lifted.

The Third Return (Ages 86–90): The Wisdom of the Soul

The final Saturn Return is a rare and sacred threshold. It represents the full integration of a human life. At this stage, Saturn is no longer a taskmaster but a silent witness to a life well-lived. This return is about spiritual culmination and the preparation for the final boundary—the transition beyond the physical world.

Saturn Through the Elements: Your Style of Discipline

The sign Saturn occupies in your chart tells us *how* you handle responsibility and where you are most likely to feel "tested."

Saturn Element	The Challenge	The Mastery
Fire (Aries, Leo, Sag)	Struggle with patience and "burning out."	Developing sustained, disciplined inspiration.
Earth (Taurus, Virgo, Cap)	Fear of poverty or material failure.	Mastery of the physical world and tangible legacy.
Air (Gemini, Libra, Aqua)	Struggle with "analysis paralysis" or social coldness.	Developing authoritative knowledge and clear logic.
Water (Cancer, Scor, Pis)	Fear of emotional vulnerability or "drowning."	Emotional resilience and the ability to hold space for others.

The Psychological Process:
Contraction vs. Expansion

Saturn works through **Contraction**. While Jupiter (which we will study later) wants to expand and say "yes" to everything, Saturn says "no" to the trivial so that you can say "yes" to the essential.

Think of Saturn as the "pruning" of a fruit tree. To the tree, the pruning feels like a loss—it is a cutting away of branches. But the gardener knows that without this contraction, the tree's energy would be wasted on leaves, and it would never produce fruit. During your Saturn Return, you are being pruned. It feels like a loss of freedom, but it is actually a concentration of power.

Saturn in the Houses:
Where the Exam Takes Place

The House placement of Saturn indicates the specific "department" of your life where you will be tested most rigorously.

- **Saturn in the 1st:** Tests of self-image and physical vitality.
- **Saturn in the 4th:** Tests regarding home, roots, and parental "debt."
- **Saturn in the 7th:** Tests of commitment, partnership, and contractual integrity.
- **Saturn in the 10th:** Tests of public reputation, career authority, and social standing.

How to "Survive" Your Saturn Return

The "secret" to Saturn is **Integrity**. Saturn is the planet of gravity; it only pulls down what isn't properly supported.

1. **Face the Facts:** Stop avoiding the bank statement, the difficult conversation, or the health check-up. Saturn rewards realism.
2. **Accept Limitations:** You cannot do everything. Choose the one thing that matters most and give it your full discipline.
3. **Show Up for the Work:** Saturn is the only planet that rewards "grind." The effort you put in during these three years will become the rock-solid foundation for the next twenty-nine.

Mini-Workbook: The Saturn Audit

1. **The Age Factor:** Are you currently approaching a Saturn Return (Ages 27, 56, or 85)? If so, what is the "loudest" problem in your life right now?

   ____

   ____

   ____

2. **The Pruning:** What is one habit, relationship, or belief you feel you are "outgrowing," even though it's painful to let go?

   ____

   ____

   ____

3. **The Authority:** In what area of life do you want people to take you seriously? (e.g., your art, your parenting, your technical skill). This is your "Saturn Goal."

   ____

   ____

   ____

Chapter 2: Transits and Timing

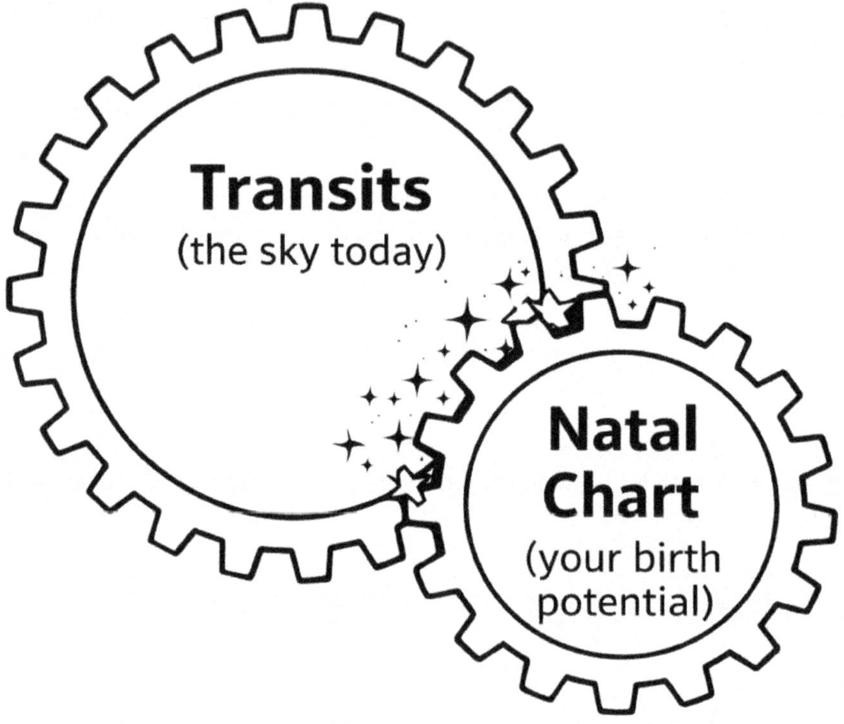

Working with Current Planetary Movements to Choose the Right Time for Action

The word "transit" simply refers to the ongoing movement of the planets as they travel through the zodiac today. At the moment you were born, the planets were "frozen" in a specific snapshot: your natal chart. However, in the sky above us, the planets never stopped moving.

A **Transit** occurs when a planet currently in the sky (the "transiting" planet) forms a mathematical relationship with a planet in your "frozen" birth chart. Think of your natal chart as a piano and the transiting planets as the fingers of a pianist. When a transiting planet "touches" a point in your chart, it "plays" that part of your personality, bringing it to the forefront of your life.

The Speed of Change: Inner vs. Outer Transits

Not all transits are created equal. The speed at which a planet moves determines how long its influence will last and how "deep" the impact will be.

- **The Inner Planets (Fast-Moving):** These include the Moon, Mercury, Venus, and Mars. Their transits last from a few hours to a few weeks. They represent the "daily weather": fleeting moods, quick conversations, minor cravings, or short-term bursts of energy. They are excellent for timing short-term actions like sending an email or going on a first date.

- **The Outer Planets (Slow-Moving):** These include Jupiter, Saturn, Uranus, Neptune, and Pluto. Their transits can last from several months to several years. These are the "climatic shifts." They represent the major chapters of your life—career changes, deep psychological transformations, and long-term relationships.

The Nature of the Transit:
The Five Major Contacts

When a transiting planet reaches a specific degree in the sky, it interacts with your birth chart through "aspects." These are the conversations between the current moment and your past.

Aspect	The Experience	The Action Required
Conjunction (0°)	A "New Beginning." Fusion of energies.	Initiate something new in that area of life.
Sextile (60°)	Opportunity and "Flow."	Say "Yes" to invitations; take a small risk.
Square (90°)	Friction and "Challenge."	Confront the obstacle; do not ignore the tension.
Trine (120°)	Ease and "Harmony."	Enjoy the rewards; things happen naturally.

Aspect	The Experience	The Action Required
Opposition (180°)	"Awareness" and Relationship.	Find balance; see the other person's perspective.

Strategic Timing: When to Act and When to Wait

Understanding transits allows you to stop fighting against the current. Here is how to use specific planetary "windows":

- **The Jupiter Window (The Green Light):** When Jupiter transits a sensitive point in your chart, it is time for **expansion.** This is the "luckiest" time to launch a business, travel, or seek a promotion. Jupiter brings confidence and growth.

- **The Mars Window (The Engine):** When Mars transits your chart, you feel a surge of physical energy and ambition. This is the time to start a fitness regime or tackle a difficult project that requires courage.

- **The Mercury Retrograde (The Pause):** We have all heard of Mercury Retrograde. In transit terms, this is when the "messenger" planet appears to move backward. This is a time for **Review, Research, and Revision.** It is not the time for new contracts, but it is the perfect time to fix what is broken.

The Transit Cycle: Knowing Where You Are

Every planet has a cycle. For example, Jupiter returns to its natal spot every 12 years. This means that at ages 12, 24, 36, 48, and 60, you experience a "Jupiter Return": a year of major opportunity and growth. By tracking these cycles, you can anticipate when your "harvest" years are coming and when you should be "planting" your seeds in silence.

Mini-Workbook: The Transit Tracker

To fill this out, use a transit app (like TimePassages or Astro-Seek) to see where the planets are today.

1. **The Current Moon:** What sign is the Moon in today? How does the "element" of that sign (Fire, Earth, Air, or Water) match your mood?

    ____

    ____

    ____

2. **The Jupiter Search:** Look for the planet Jupiter (♃) in the sky right now. Which "House" in your natal chart is it currently traveling through? (Example: If it's in your 2nd House, you may see changes in your finances).

    ____

    ____

    ____

3. **The Retrograde Check:** Are any planets currently retrograde (marked with an R_x)? If so, what area of your life feels like it is "on hold" or requires a second look?

    ____

    ____

    ____

Chapter 3: Relationship Synastry

Comparing Charts to See How Your Energy Interacts with Others

In the practice of astrology, **Synastry** is the technical study of how two people affect one another. It is the process of overlaying one person's birth chart onto another's to see where the planets "land." If you have ever felt an inexplicable sense of safety with a stranger, or a sudden, sharp irritation toward someone you barely know, you are experiencing the mechanics of synastry.

Relationships are not just about "compatibility"; they are about **resonance.** Synastry does not tell you if a relationship is "good" or "bad." Instead, it identifies where the relationship will feel like a warm breeze (harmonious aspects) and where it will feel like a heavy lift (challenging aspects). By understanding these "pressure points," we can move from reactive conflict to conscious partnership.

The Three Pillars of Connection

When comparing two charts, astrologers look for three primary types of connections that define the "flavor" of the bond:

1. The Luminaries: The Emotional Core

The most important connections involve the Sun and the Moon.

- **Sun-Sun:** This describes the "vitality" of the pair. Do your core identities support or compete with one another?

- **Moon-Moon:** This is the "comfort level." If your Moons are in compatible elements (e.g., Water and Earth), you will likely feel "at home" with one another. If they are in clashing signs, you may struggle to understand each other's emotional needs.

2. The Personal Planets: Communication and Chemistry

- **Mercury-Mercury:** This governs how you talk. A strong Mercury connection means you "get" each other's jokes and logic.

- **Venus-Mars:** This is the classic "chemistry" axis. Venus represents what we find beautiful and how we love; Mars represents how we pursue and our physical drive. When your Venus touches their Mars (or vice versa), the spark is often immediate and undeniable.

3. The House Overlays: The "Room" You Occupy

When your planets "fall" into your partner's houses, it determines the role you play in their life.

- If your Sun falls in their **7th House**, you are their primary partner.

- If your Sun falls in their **10th House**, you act as a mentor or influence their career.

- If your Sun falls in their **4th House**, you feel like family, regardless of your actual relation.

The Role of the Nodes: Karmic Contracts

As we discussed in **Book 2**, the Lunar Nodes represent our destiny and growth. In synastry, connections to the Nodes are often called "Karmic."

- **North Node Connections:** These relationships feel like they are "going somewhere." They pull you toward your future and can be intensely growth-oriented, though not always easy.

- **South Node Connections:** These feel instantly familiar—the "I've known you forever" sensation. While comfortable, these bonds can sometimes keep you stuck in old habits if you aren't careful.

Navigating "Hard" Synastry

A common mistake is fearing "squares" or "oppositions" in synastry. While these aspects create friction, friction is what creates heat and movement. A relationship with only "easy" trines might eventually become stagnant or boring.

- **Saturn Connections:** Often called the "Cosmic Glue." While Saturn can feel heavy or restrictive, it is the planet that provides the commitment necessary for a relationship to last twenty years instead of twenty days.

- **Uranus Connections:** These provide the excitement and the "break from the norm," but can be unstable if not grounded by other planets.

The Composite Chart: The "Third Person"

While synastry looks at how *Person A* affects *Person B*, the **Composite Chart** is a mathematical midpoint of both charts. It represents the relationship itself as its own living entity. If the relationship were a person, what would its personality be?

- A composite Sun in the **1st House** makes for a very "public" couple.

- A composite Sun in the **12th House** might indicate a very private or spiritually focused bond.

Mini-Workbook: The Relationship Audit

For this exercise, you will need your chart and the chart of a close friend, partner, or family member.

1. **The Elemental Match:** What is your dominant element? What is theirs? (Example: You are Air; they are Fire). How does this play out? Does the "Fire" heat up the "Air," or does the "Air" blow out the "Fire"?

    ____

    ____

    ____

2. **The Venus Discovery:** Look at your Venus sign. Now look at the House it occupies in *their* chart. (Example: Your Venus is in their 11th House of Friendship). What does this tell you about the "role" you play for them?

____

____

____

3. **The Tension Point:** Identify one recurring argument or misunderstanding. Looking at your charts, is there a "Square" (90°) or "Opposition" (180°) between your Mercury and theirs?

____

____

____

Chapter 4: Midheaven and Career

Locating Your Highest Point in the Sky to Find Vocational Clarity

The **Midheaven**, or *Medium Coeli* (Latin for "Middle of the Sky"), is often abbreviated as the **MC**. It is the point where the ecliptic intersects the local meridian at the time of your birth. Visually, it represents the sun at high noon: the moment when it is most visible, most powerful, and casting the shortest shadow.

In your birth chart, the MC represents your **Public Persona.** While your Ascendant is the "mask" you wear when meeting someone for the first time, your MC is the "mask" you wear for the world. It governs your career, your social status, your relationship with authority, and your ultimate professional aspirations.

The MC vs. the IC: The Tree and the Roots

To understand the Midheaven, you must understand its opposite point: the **Imum Coeli (IC)**, or "Bottom of the Sky."

- **The IC (4th House):** This is your private life, your home, your ancestry, and your internal emotional foundation. It is the root system of the tree.

- **The MC (10th House):** This is the fruit of the tree. It is what the public sees.

A healthy career (MC) cannot exist without a stable private life (IC). If your Midheaven is in Leo, you may crave a career in the spotlight, but if your IC is in Aquarius, your "roots" are in intellectual detachment and independence. You must use that independence as a foundation to support your public Leo leadership.

The Midheaven Through the Elements: Your Vocational "Why"

The sign on your Midheaven describes the *quality* of the work you are meant to do and how the public perceives you.

MC Element	The Professional Vibe	Ideal Work Environment
Fire (Ari, Leo, Sag)	The Pioneer/Leader. Needs visibility and action.	Entrepreneurship, performance, high-stakes leadership.
Earth (Tau, Vir, Cap)	The Builder/Manager. Needs tangible results.	Finance, architecture, administration, craftsmanship.
Air (Gem, Lib, Aqu)	The Communicator/Networker. Needs social exchange.	Media, law, education, technology, public relations.

MC Element	The Professional Vibe	Ideal Work Environment
Water (Can, Sco, Pis)	The Healer/Intuitive. Needs emotional depth.	Counseling, art, healthcare, social work, non-profits.

Planets Conjunct the Midheaven: The Professional Flavor

Any planet sitting close to your MC (within 8–10 degrees) acts as a "co-pilot" for your career.

- **Mars on the MC:** You are seen as competitive and driven. You may thrive in high-pressure environments.

- **Venus on the MC:** You are seen as charming and artistic. Your career may involve beauty, harmony, or mediation.

- **Saturn on the MC:** You are seen as a serious authority figure. Career success often comes later in life through hard work.

- **Neptune on the MC:** Your career path may be unconventional, creative, or spiritual, but potentially lacking in clear boundaries.

Navigating Career Transits

Because the MC is a "mathematical point" rather than a physical body, it is extremely sensitive to transits.

- **Jupiter transiting your MC:** This is a major "Expansion" year for your career. It often brings promotions, awards, or the successful launch of a business.

- **Saturn transiting your MC:** This is a "Consolidation" year. You may feel more weight or responsibility. It is a time for professional auditing—cutting away what doesn't work to build a more solid reputation.

Mini-Workbook: The Vocational Map

1. **Locate your MC:** Look at the vertical line at the top of your chart. What sign is it in? (e.g., MC in Gemini).

    ----

2. **The Public Perception:** Read the element description above for your MC sign. Does this "Professional Vibe" match how people describe you at work? Or do you feel you are currently working in an environment that clacks with this energy?

    ----

3. **The Planetary Influence:** Do you have any planets in your 10th house or touching your MC line? If so, list them. How might these planets be "coloring" your professional ambitions?

Chapter 5: Progressions and Inner Growth

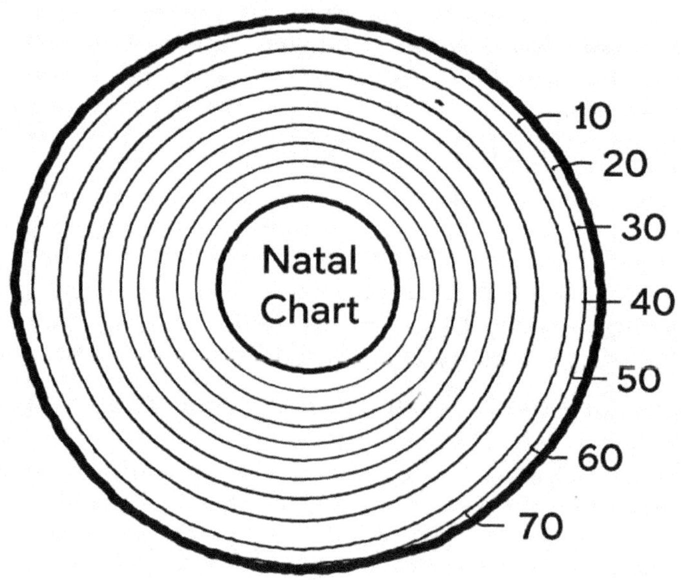

How Your Chart Evolves as You Age

The technical foundation of progressions is based on a symbolic formula: **"A Day for a Year."** In this system, the movements of the planets during the first 90 days of your life correspond to the first 90 years of your life. For example, the position of the planets on the 30th day after your birth describes the internal "climate" of your 30th year.

If your Natal Chart is the **seed** (the DNA of who you are), Progressions are the **tree** (how that DNA unfolds over time). You don't "lose" your birth chart, but you "grow into" new versions of yourself. This explains why a person born with the Sun in a quiet sign like Pisces might suddenly become more assertive and ambitious in their 30s as their Progressed Sun moves into Aries.

The Progressed Moon: Your Emotional Seasons

The most significant progression for most people is the **Secondary Progressed Moon.** Because the Moon moves quickly, its progression is palpable. It takes approximately **27 to 28 years** to move through the entire zodiac.

Every 2.5 years, your Progressed Moon moves into a new sign and a new house. This marks a shift in your "emotional focus."

- **Progressed Moon in the 1st House:** A time of rebirth and focusing on your own needs.

- **Progressed Moon in the 10th House:** A season where your heart is in your work and public achievement.

- **Progressed Moon in the 12th House:** A period of "hermiting," withdrawal, and spiritual preparation before a new 28-year cycle begins.

The Progressed Sun:
Changing Your Core Identity

Unlike the Moon, the **Progressed Sun** moves very slowly—only one degree per year. This means that at some point in your life (usually between birth and age 30), your Progressed Sun will move into the next zodiac sign.

When your Sun "changes signs" by progression, it feels like a fundamental shift in your core vitality. You begin to adopt the traits of the new sign to help fulfill the goals of your original natal sign.

- **Example:** A Gemini Sun (Air/Communicator) progresses into Cancer (Water/Nurturer). The person remains a Gemini, but their way of communicating becomes more emotional, protective, and focused on home and family.

The Progressed Lunation Cycle

Just as there is a New Moon and a Full Moon in the sky every month, there is a **Progressed Lunation Cycle** that lasts about 29 years.

- **Progressed New Moon:** A time of "darkness" where a new life chapter is being seeded. You may feel directionless, but you are actually preparing for a major 30-year journey.

- **Progressed Full Moon (Approx. 14 years later):** The "high point" of the cycle. This is when the seeds planted at the New Moon come into full bloom. It is often a time of great clarity or public recognition.

Why Progressions Matter for Decision-Making

Understanding your progressions prevents you from judging yourself for "changing." If you were a social butterfly in your 20s but find yourself craving solitude and spiritual depth in your 30s, it is likely that a major progression (like the Moon entering the 8th or 12th house) is occurring. Progressions give you **permission to evolve.**

Mini-Workbook: The Evolution Audit

To answer these, you will need to generate a "Secondary Progressions" chart on a site like Astro.com or Astro-Seek.

1. **The Current Moon Phase:** What sign is your **Progressed Moon** in right now? Look back 2.5 years; did your emotional priorities change significantly when the Moon entered this sign?

   ____

   ____

2. **The Core Shift:** In what year did (or will) your **Progressed Sun** change signs? If it has already happened, what major personality shift did you notice during that three-year window?

   ____

   ____

3. **The House Focus:** Which House is your Progressed Moon currently traveling through? (e.g., the 2nd House of Money/Values). How does this match your current "inner preoccupation"?

   ____

   ____

Conclusion:
Living in Sync with Natural Cycles

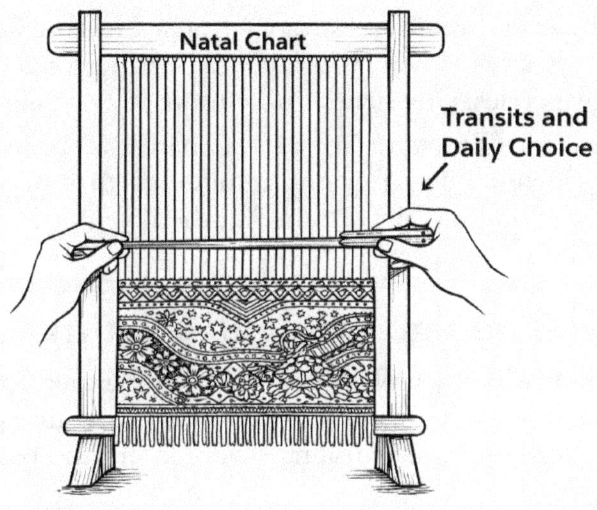

The Return to Rhythmic Wisdom

In our modern world, we are conditioned to believe that we should be productive, social, and "on" at all times. We treat the year as a flat line of 365 identical days. However, as you have discovered through the lens of astrology, time is not flat, it is a spiral.

To live in sync with natural cycles is to accept that there is a season for everything under the sun. There is a season for **Saturnian contraction**, where you must work hard, set boundaries, and face reality. There is a season for **Jupiterian expansion**, where you should say "yes" to the unknown and take up more space. There is a season for **Mercury-driven revision**, and a season for **Lunar-driven rest**.

When you stop trying to force a "Summer" activity in a "Winter" transit, the exhaustion and anxiety of modern life begin to lift. You realize that "delays" are often just the universe's way of ensuring you are properly prepared for the next step.

The Three Keys to Cosmic Navigation

As you conclude **Book 3**, keep these three principles as your compass:

1. **Awareness over Anxiety:** Use the transits not to predict the future with fear, but to prepare for it with awareness. If you know a challenging transit is coming, you don't hide; you fortify.

2. **Integrity over Impulse:** Astrology teaches us that we are part of a larger system. When you align your personal will with the collective cycles, your actions have more weight and more integrity.

3. **Patience over Pressure:** Your birth chart is a promise that unfolds over a lifetime. Progressions remind us that we are constantly ripening. You don't need to be "finished" yet; you only need to be in your current season.

The End of the Beginning

This book has provided you with the "Purpose Planner" for your current year, but the real work begins now. Every day is a conversation between your natal potential and the transiting sky. You are the conductor of this orchestra.

You have moved from being someone who "has a sign" to being someone who "lives a chart." You have the tools to navigate career shifts, relationship changes, and personal crises with a sense of perspective that only the stars can provide.

Reflection Questions:
Planning Your Purposeful Year

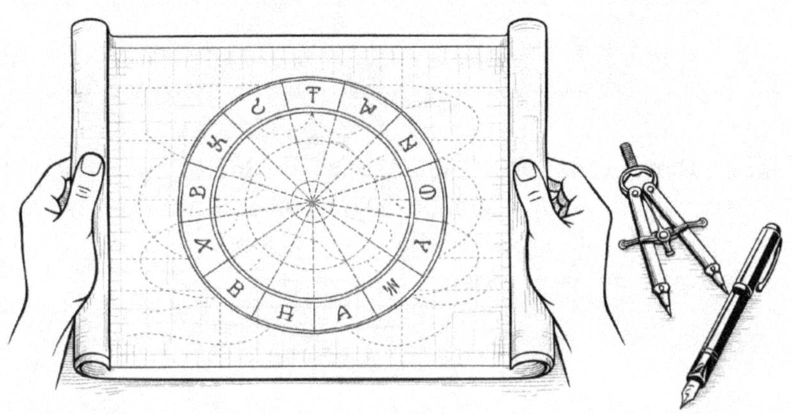

Layer 1: The Saturn Maturity Audit

1. **Defining the Work:** Identify which "House" Saturn is currently transiting in your chart. (e.g., if Saturn is in your 2nd House, your focus is on financial discipline). What is one specific, "boring" responsibility in this area that you have been avoiding?

   ____

   ____

   ____

2. **The Threshold:** If you are within three years of a Saturn Return (Ages 27–30, 56–60, or 85–88), what major "childish" habit are you being asked to trade in for a more "adult" commitment?

   ____

   ____

   ____

Layer 2: The Transit Strategy

3. **The Jupiter Leap:** Locate where transiting Jupiter is currently in your chart. This is your "Green Light" zone. If you were guaranteed not to fail, what one big risk would you take in this area of your life right now?

____

____

____

____

4. **The Retrograde Review:** Think back to the last Mercury Retrograde. What "glitches" or communication breakdowns occurred? Looking back, what was the universe trying to get you to slow down and re-examine?

____

____

____

____

Layer 3: The Internal Ripening (Progressions)

5. **The Progressed Moon Phase:** Is your Progressed Moon currently in a "Visible" house (7–12) or a "Private" house (1–6)? How does this match your current level of social energy? Are you fighting a need for solitude, or resisting a call to step onto the stage?

____

____

____

____

6. **The Evolving Self:** If your Progressed Sun has changed signs in the last five years, how has your "core drive" shifted? (e.g., moving from a focus on security to a focus on communication).

____

____

____

____

Layer 4: The Vocational Legacy (Midheaven)

7. **Public vs. Private:** Does your current job title reflect the energy of your Midheaven sign? If not, what is one small way you can start "acting" like your MC sign in your professional interactions?

____

____

____

____

The 12-Month Purpose Planner

Quarter	Major Transit/Progression	My Primary Goal
Q1		
Q2		
Q3		
Q4		

Workbook Section 3: The Purpose Planner

Part 1: The Annual Transit Calendar

Using a transit generator (such as Astro-Seek or TimePassages), identify the "High Stakes" dates for the current year. This is not about predicting events, but about identifying the **Energetic Climate** you will be working within.

Q1: The Foundation (January – March)

- **Major Saturn Aspect:** ______________________________
- **Mercury Retrograde Dates:** ______________________________
- **Personal Goal:** (Focus on discipline and structural integrity)

____

____

Q2: The Expansion (April – June)

- **Major Jupiter Aspect:** ______________________________
- **Mars House Placement:** ______________________________
- **Personal Goal:** (Focus on risk-taking and visibility)

____

____

____

Q3: The Internalization (July – September)

- **Progressed Moon Phase:** ______________________________
- **Outer Planet Retrogrades:** ______________________________
- **Personal Goal:** (Focus on review, rest, and internal ripening)

____

____

____

____

Q4: The Culmination (October – December)

- **Sun/MC Aspects:** ____
- **End-of-Year Transits:** ____________________________________
- **Personal Goal:** (Focus on harvest and public standing)

    ____

    ____

Part 2: The Vocation Worksheet (Midheaven Alignment)

This worksheet bridges the gap between your current job and your soul's highest professional calling (The MC).

1. The MC Archetype

- **My Midheaven Sign:** _______________________________________
- **The "Shadow" of this Sign:** (e.g., if MC is Aries, the shadow is impulsivity/aggression)
- **The "Light" of this Sign:** (e.g., if MC is Aries, the light is pioneering leadership)

    ____

    ____

    ____

2. The Current Alignment Check

- On a scale of 1–10, how much does my current daily work allow me to express my MC Sign? _________________________________
- What is one specific task I perform that feels **drained** and "un-aligned"?

    ____

    ____

    ____

- What is one specific task I perform that feels **energized** and "on-purpose"?

    ____

    ____

    ____

3. The Public Legacy Goal

If you were to receive a "Lifetime Achievement Award" ten years from now, what would the inscription on the award say based on your Midheaven's potential?

"Awarded to [Your Name] for their [Adjective/Sign-based trait] contribution to the field of [Vocation/Topic]."

Part 3: The Progression Tracker (Internal Ripening)

While transits are the "News," progressions are the "Novel." Document your current internal chapter.

- **Current Progressed Moon Sign:** ______________________________
- **Current Progressed Moon House:** ______________________________
- **The Theme of this Chapter:** (e.g., "The Year of Financial Security" or "The Year of Learning to Speak My Truth")
- **The Next Shift:** When does my Moon move into the next sign?

  ____

  ____

- **The Preparation:** What must I finish in my current "Emotional Season" before I am ready for the next one?

  ____

  ____

Part 4: The Strategic Integration (Final Review)

Look at your findings from **Book 1** (The Map), **Book 2** (The Identity), and **Book 3** (The Timing). Write your **Strategic Command** for the next twelve months:

"Because I am naturally [Book 1 Element/Modality] and my soul's path is [Book 2 North Node], I will utilize the current transit of [Planet] through my [House] to achieve [Book 3 Career Goal]. I will honor my [Progressed Moon] need for [Emotion] while stepping into my [Midheaven] role as a [Archetype]."

Overall Conclusion: The Symphony of the Self

The Final Synthesis: From Data to Wisdom

We began this journey in **Book 1** by deconstructing the sky into its fundamental parts: the planets, the houses, and the geometric relationships we call aspects. In **Book 2**, we breathed life into those parts, identifying the unique "energetic signature" that distinguishes you from everyone else born on your day. Finally, in **Book 3**, we set that identity in motion, learning to dance with the rhythmic cycles of time.

As you stand at the end of this curriculum, the goal is no longer to "read" a chart as if it were a technical manual or a static set of instructions. The goal is to **inhabit** your chart. Astrology, at its highest level, is not a system of belief; it is a language of perception. It provides a framework through which we can view the chaotic events of our lives as meaningful movements in a larger, purposeful symphony.

The Paradox of Fate and Free Will

One of the most profound realizations that comes from studying your own "Cosmic Identity" is the resolution of the tension between fate and free will. Many beginners fear that astrology implies a "fixed" life where choice is an illusion. However, as you have seen through the study of transits and progressions, the stars do not compel; they impel.

Think of your birth chart as the **hulk of a ship** and the transits as the **ocean currents.** You did not choose the ship you were born with; some are built for speed, others for heavy cargo, some for shallow waters, and others for the deep sea. You also do not choose the weather of the day. However, you are the absolute master of the **sails.** A "difficult" Saturn transit is not a sentence of suffering; it is a heavy sea that demands you tighten your riggings and focus your discipline. A "lucky" Jupiter transit is a following wind that rewards those who are brave enough to unfurl every inch of canvas. Astrology doesn't take away your choice; it gives you the data necessary to make your choices effective.

The Ethics of the "Knower"

As you move forward with this knowledge, you carry a new responsibility. Understanding the birth charts of others, your partners, children, and colleagues, gives you a "backstage pass" to their psychological machinery.

Authoritative astrology must always be practiced with **Humility and Compassion.** * **The Trap of Labeling:** Never use astrology to put someone in a box. Avoid saying, *"You're a Gemini, so you can't be trusted,"* or *"I have Chiron in the 7th, so I'm destined for heartbreak."* These are misuses of the language.

- **The Gift of Empathy:** Instead, use your knowledge to say, *"I see that you have a high Air score, so I understand why you need intellectual space,"* or *"I recognize my own Saturn pressure, so I will be patient with my own slow progress."*

The purpose of this work is **Individuation,** the process of becoming the most authentic version of yourself, inclusive of your "shadow" and your "light."

The Living Sky: Your Ongoing Dialogue

The conclusion of these books is not the end of your education; it is the beginning of a lifelong dialogue with the cosmos. The sky is never silent. Every night, the planets move into new configurations, sparking new insights and challenges within your natal potential.

You are now equipped with the "Grammar of the Stars." You can look at a world event or a personal crisis and ask: *"Which archetype is speaking here? Is this a Martian call to courage? A Neptunian call to surrender? A Plutonian call to rebirth?"* When you can name the energy, you are no longer a victim of it. You become a co-creator with the universe. You understand that your life is not a series of random accidents, but a narrative being written in the ink of light and time.

Final Words of Encouragement

As you close this volume and step back into the world, do so with the confidence of someone who knows their "True North." You have mapped your elements, found your signature, faced your wounds, and planned your future.

The stars have been watching over humanity for millions of years, providing a map for the lost and a clock for the weary. By engaging with this ancient wisdom, you have joined a long lineage of seekers who refused to believe that human life is insignificant. You are a microcosm of the macrocosm. The same iron in your blood was forged in the hearts of dying stars; the same rhythm that moves the tides moves your emotions.

You are not just **in** the universe; you **are** the universe experiencing itself through a specific, unique, and beautiful lens. Go forth and live your chart with courage, integrity, and wonder.

The Print and Keep Checklist: A Quick-Reference Guide

Step 1: The Cosmic Triage (The Essentials)

Before looking at specific placements, assess the "Big Three" to understand the framework of the personality.

- **The Sun Sign:** (The Core Identity). What is the fuel? What does this person need to feel "alive"?

- **The Moon Sign:** (The Emotional Body). How do they process safety? What is their private "home" state?

- **The Ascendant (Rising):** (The Social Mask). How do they meet the world? What is their immediate physical presence?

Step 2: The Temperament Audit (Scores)

Calculate the elemental and modal balance to find the "Signature Sign."

- **Elements:** Count planets in Fire, Earth, Air, and Water. Which is the "Void" (missing) and which is the "Dominant"?

- **Modalities:** Count planets in Cardinal, Fixed, and Mutable. Is this person a Starter, a Sustainer, or an Adapter?

- **Signature Sign:** Combine the Dominant Element and Dominant Modality (e.g., Water + Fixed = Scorpio Signature).

Step 3: The Evolutionary Compass

Look for the direction of growth and the points of internal resistance.

- **The North Node:** Identify the sign and house. This is the "Learning Curve"—the unfamiliar but rewarding path.

- **The South Node:** Identify the opposite sign/house. This is the "Comfort Zone"—the talent that can become a trap.

- **Chiron:** Locate the "Wounded Healer." Where does this person feel an irrational insecurity that eventually becomes their greatest wisdom?

Step 4: The Public Standing (Vocational Check)

Look to the highest point of the chart to see how they are "seen" by the world.

- **The Midheaven (MC):** Identify the sign. What is their professional "vibe"?

- **The 10th House:** Are there any planets sitting here? These are the "Co-pilots" of their career.

Step 5: The Dynamic Timing (Current Windows)

Apply the "Day-to-Day" layer to the "Life" layer.

- **Saturn's Position:** Where is the "Great Teacher" currently applying pressure?

- **Jupiter's Position:** Where is the "Great Expander" currently offering a green light?

- **Mercury Retrograde:** Is it currently active? (If so, focus on "Re" activities—Review, Repair, Reflect).

Quick Interpretation Cheat Sheet

Factor	Fire	Earth	Air	Water
Needs...	Action / Inspiration	Stability / Touch	Ideas / Connection	Depth / Intimacy
Avoids...	Boredom	Chaos	Isolation	Superficiality

Modality	Cardinal	Fixed	Mutable
Goal	To Initiate	To Maintain	To Change
Stress Response	Taking Charge	Digging In	Shapeshifting

Pro-Tip for Chart Readers

"Synthesize, Don't Just List." > A chart is not a grocery list; it is a recipe. Don't just say, "You have a Moon in Aries and a Sun in Capricorn." Say, "You have an ambitious Capricorn core that is fueled by an emotionally impulsive Aries heart." Look for the **and** that connects the contradictions.

If you enjoyed this book, I'd greatly appreciate a review on Amazon because it helps me to create more books that people want. It would mean a lot to hear from you.

To leave a review:

1. Open your camera app.
2. Point your mobile device at the QR code.
3. The review page will appear in your web browser.

____

Thanks for your support!

Here's another book by Mari Silva that you might like

Your Free Gift
(only available for a limited time)

Thanks for getting this book! If you want to learn more about various spirituality topics, then join Mari Silva's community and get a free guided meditation MP3 for awakening your third eye. This guided meditation mp3 is designed to open and strengthen ones third eye so you can experience a higher state of consciousness. Simply visit the link below the image to get started.

https://spiritualityspot.com/meditation

Or, Scan the QR code!

Resource List

Overall Introduction

Printed Books and Academic Texts

- **Hunger, H., & Pingree, D. (1989).** *MUL.APIN: An Astronomical Compendium in Cuneiform.* Archiv für Orientforschung. (The definitive translation and analysis of the earliest Babylonian celestial records).

- **Jung, C. G. (1971).** *Psychological Types (Collected Works of C.G. Jung, Vol. 6).* Princeton University Press. (Foundational text for understanding archetypal theory and personality frameworks).

- **Jung, C. G. (2012).** *Jung on Astrology.* (Edited by Safron Rossi and Keiron Le Grice). Routledge. (A collection of Jung's letters and writings specifically regarding his use of astrology in clinical psychology).

- **Koch-Westenholz, U. (1995).** *Mesopotamian Astrology: An Introduction to Babylonian and Assyrian Celestial Divination.* Museum Tusculanum Press. (Explores the transition of astrology from a state-level tool to an individual practice).

Scientific Studies and Journals

- **Gonda, X., et al. (2014).** "Season of birth variations in the temperament and character inventory of personality in a general population." *European College of Neuropsychopharmacology.* (A study linking birth season to dopamine and serotonin turnover and long-term mood patterns).

- **Pantazatos, S. P. (2014).** "Season of birth is associated with a brain structure–personality correlation." *NeuroImage / Wired.* (Research exploring how grey matter volume in specific brain regions correlates with the time of year an individual is born).

- **Vanderbilt University (2010).** "Season of birth may have long-term effects on personality, study suggests." *ScienceDaily.* (A report on biological clock "imprinting" based on light cycles at the time of birth).

Digital Resources

- **NASA Eclipse Web Site:** (https://eclipse.gsfc.nasa.gov) – Reliable data for verifying historical celestial events and planetary cycles.

- **The British Museum Cuneiform Collection:** (https://www.britishmuseum.org) – Digital archives of the *MUL.APIN* tablets and other Mesopotamian astronomical artifacts.

- **PubMed / National Center for Biotechnology Information:** (https://pubmed.ncbi.nlm.nih.gov) – Searchable database for peer-reviewed studies on chronobiology and "season of birth" effects on human physiology.

Book 1

Introduction

Printed Books

- **Arroyo, S. (1975).** *Astrology, Psychology, and the Four Elements.* CRCS Publications. (Explores the integration of psychological principles with traditional astrological theory).

- **Hand, R. (1981).** *Horoscope Symbols.* Para Research. (A comprehensive guide to the technical and symbolic meaning of planetary placements).

- **Plato.** *Timaeus.* (Various editions). (The classical philosophical text regarding the "World Soul" and celestial order).

- **Tarnas, R. (2006).** *Cosmos and Psyche: Intimations of a New World View.* Viking Press. (A scholarly look at the correlation between planetary transits and world history).

Scientific and Technical Resources

- **Condon, N. C., et al. (2010).** "Season of Birth Imprints the Mammalian Circadian Clock." *Nature Neuroscience.* (Research on how birth timing affects biological rhythms and personality traits).

- **Swiss Ephemeris:** (https://www.astro.com/swisseph/sweph_e.htm) – The professional standard for high-precision astronomical calculations used in astrology software.

- **The Project Hindsight Archives:** (http://www.projecthindsight.com) – A collection of translated Hellenistic astrological texts that define the origins of horoscopic astrology.

Chapter 1

Printed Books

- **Ptolemy, C.** *Tetrabiblos.* (Various translations). (The foundational text for the significations of the houses and planetary strength).
- **Sasportas, H. (1985).** *The Twelve Houses.* Aquarian Press. (A modern classic that explores the psychological and practical meanings of each house).
- **Vaughan, V. (2018).** *Houses: The Architecture of the Human Experience.* (An authoritative look at the technical history of house division systems).
- **Whitfield, P. (2001).** *Astrology: A History.* British Library. (Explores the evolution of the chart wheel and its mathematical foundations).

Scientific and Historical Resources

- **The Arhat Publications:** (http://www.robhand.com) – Led by Robert Hand, this project translates and preserves ancient texts regarding house systems and Hellenistic techniques.
- **The History of Science Museum, Oxford:** (https://www.hsm.ox.ac.uk) – Provides digital records of astrolabes and early tools used to calculate the houses before modern computing.
- **National Center for Geocosmic Research (NCGR):** (https://geocosmic.org) – An educational organization that provides technical papers on the mathematics of house division (Placidus vs. Koch vs. Whole Sign).

Chapter 2

Printed Books

- **Campbell, J. (1949).** *The Hero with a Thousand Faces.* Pantheon Books. (The definitive work on the Hero's Journey, essential for understanding the Sun's archetypal role).
- **Greene, L. (1977).** *Relating: An Astrological Guide to Living with Others on a Small Planet.* Samuel Weiser. (A deep psychological exploration of the Sun/Moon dynamic in relationships).
- **Leo, A. (1912).** *The Key to Your Own Nativity.* (A historical text that helped popularize the importance of the Ascendant in modern readings).

- **Tarnas, R. (2006).** *Cosmos and Psyche.* Viking. (Provides historical context for how planetary alignments mirror psychological states).

Technical and Academic Resources

- **The Journal of Consciousness Studies:** (https://www.ingentaconnect.com/content/imp/jcs) – Peer-reviewed articles on the nature of the ego and subconscious, providing a scientific backdrop for Sun/Moon theory.

- **The Gauquelin Data Archive:** (http://www.curtismanwaring.com/gauquelin/) – Research by Michel Gauquelin regarding the statistical prominence of certain planets (like the Moon) near the angles of the birth chart.

- **Astro-Databank:** (https://www.astro.com/astro-databank) – A vast database of verified birth times to study how the Ascendant manifests in public figures.

Chapter 3

Printed Books

- **Greene, L. (1984).** *The Astrology of Fate.* Samuel Weiser. (Contains deep analysis of the mythic archetypes of the inner planets).

- **Moore, T. (1992).** *Care of the Soul.* HarperCollins. (A psychological look at how we value things, reflecting Venusian themes).

- **Tierney, B. (1983).** *Dynamics of Aspect Analysis.* CRCS Publications. (Provides technical details on how Mercury, Venus, and Mars interact in the chart).

- **Vaughan, V. (1994).** *The Personal Planets.* (A focused look at the astronomical and psychological roles of the inner trio).

Technical and Academic Resources

- **The American Federation of Astrologers (AFA):** (https://www.astrologers.com) – Provides technical papers on the calculation of planetary speed and its effect on personality.

- **The C.G. Jung Institute, Zurich:** (https://junginstitut.ch) – Resources on archetypal theory and the "anima/animus" dynamics often associated with Venus and Mars.

- **NASA Planetary Fact Sheets:** (https://nssdc.gsfc.nasa.gov/planetary/factsheet/) – Objective data on the orbital cycles and distances of Mercury, Venus, and Mars from the Sun.

Chapter 4

Printed Books

- **Arroyo, S. (1996).** *Exploring Jupiter: The Astrological Key to Progress, Prosperity & Destiny.* CRCS Publications. (A thorough examination of Jupiter's role in personal growth).

- **Greene, L. (1976).** *Saturn: A New Look at an Old Devil.* Samuel Weiser. (The essential text for reframing Saturnian challenges as opportunities for mastery).

- **Hand, R. (1981).** *Essays on Astrology.* Whitford Press. (Contains technical and historical data on the discovery of the modern planets).

- **Tarnas, R. (2006).** *Cosmos and Psyche.* Viking. (A foundational scholarly work on planetary cycles and historical eras).

Technical and Academic Resources

- **The Lowell Observatory:** (https://lowell.edu) – Historical records regarding the search for "Planet X" and the eventual discovery of Pluto.

- **The International Astronomical Union (IAU):** (https://www.iau.org) – For the scientific history of planetary classification and naming conventions.

- **The Journal of Humanistic Psychology:** (https://journals.sagepub.com/home/jhp) – Provides secular research on generational cohorts that aligns with the transpersonal planetary cycles.

Chapter 5

Printed Books

- **Kepler, J.** *The Harmony of the World.* (Various translations). (The original 1619 text exploring the relationship between geometry, music, and the stars).

- **Pelletier, R. (1974).** *Planets in Aspect.* Para Research. (An authoritative encyclopedia of every possible planetary combination).

- **Tierney, B. (1983).** *Dynamics of Aspect Analysis.* CRCS Publications. (A masterclass in reading chart patterns and the "geometry" of the soul).

- **Tompkins, S. (1989).** *Aspects in Astrology: A Guide to Understanding Planetary Relationships in the Horoscope.* Destiny Books.

Technical and Academic Resources

- **The Kepler Project:** (https://www.kepler.org) – Dedicated to the preservation of Johannes Kepler's astronomical and astrological manuscripts.

- **The International Society for Astrological Research (ISAR):**
  (https://isarastrology.org) – Provides technical webinars and papers on
  the calculation and interpretation of minor and major aspects.

- **Physics World - "The Music of the Spheres":**
  (https://physicsworld.com) – Articles exploring the historical and
  mathematical link between planetary orbits and harmonic ratios.

Conclusion

Printed Books

- **Forrest, S. (1984).** *The Inner Sky: How to Make Wiser Choices for a
  More Fulfilling Life.* Seven Paws Press. (The definitive guide for
  synthesizing astrological symbols into a coherent narrative).

- **Hillman, J. (1996).** *The Soul's Code: In Search of Character and
  Calling.* Random House. (Essential for understanding the "Acorn
  Theory" and the concept of a pre-destined character blueprint).

- **Greene, L. (1980).** *A Manual of Horoscope Interpretation.* (A
  professional-level guide on how to weigh different chart factors to reach
  a final "judgment").

- **Hand, R. (1981).** *Horoscope Symbols.* Whitford Press. (A technical
  resource for understanding how to prioritize planetary strength).

Scientific and Academic Resources

- **The Archive for Research in Archetypal Symbolism (ARAS):**
  (https://aras.org) – A pictorial archive and commentary on archetypal
  symbols found in astrology and world mythology.

- **The Journal of Analytical Psychology:**
  (https://onlinelibrary.wiley.com/journal/14685922) – Peer-reviewed
  research on Jungian synthesis and the integration of personality parts.

- **Astro-Seek Synthesis Tools:** (https://www.astro-seek.com) – Provides
  automated calculations for "elemental balance" and "dominant planets"
  to aid in the synthesis process.

Reflection Questions

Printed Books

- **Greene, L. (1976).** *The Astrology of Fate.* Samuel Weiser. (A deep
  dive into the psychological concept of "resistance" to one's own chart).

- **Jung, C.G. (1959).** *The Archetypes and the Collective Unconscious.*
  Princeton University Press. (Essential for understanding the mirror
  effect of symbols).

- **Merton, T. (1955).** *No Man Is an Island.* (A philosophical look at self-
  knowledge and the importance of reflection).

Digital and Scientific Resources

- **The Greater Good Science Center (UC Berkeley):** (https://greatergood.berkeley.edu) – Provides research-based exercises on self-reflection and the benefits of self-awareness.

- **The Journal of Personality and Social Psychology:** (https://www.apa.org/pubs/journals/psp) – Studies on "Self-Verification Theory," which explains why we seek information that confirms our inner sense of self.

Workbook Section 1

- **AFA (American Federation of Astrologers):** *The Astrological Chart Data Sheets.* (Professional templates for manual chart casting).

- **Michelsen, N. F.** *The American Ephemeris for the 21st Century.* (The standard reference for finding planetary positions and degrees).

- **Astro.com / Extended Chart Selection:** Use the "Porphyry" or "Placidus" house system options to verify the degrees and house cusps recorded in your log.

Book 2

Introduction

Printed Books

- **Arroyo, S. (1998).** *Astrology, Karma & Transformation.* CRCS Publications. (A masterwork on the deeper, evolutionary meaning of the birth chart).

- **Greene, L. (1977).** *Relating: An Astrological Guide to Living with Others on a Small Planet.* Samuel Weiser. (Explores how we project our internal "Sun sign stereotypes" onto others).

- **Jung, C. G. (1921).** *Psychological Types.* (The foundational text for understanding the four functions of consciousness—Thinking, Feeling, Sensation, Intuition).

- **Tarnas, R. (2006).** *Cosmos and Psyche.* Viking. (A scholarly exploration of how planetary archetypes have shaped human history and individual identity).

Scientific and Historical Resources

- **The Archive for Research in Archetypal Symbolism (ARAS):** (https://aras.org) – A vast digital library of images and commentary on the symbols that make up our cosmic identity.

- **The Center for Psychological Astrology (CPA):** (https://www.cpalondon.com) – Provides technical papers on the integration of Jungian psychology with birth chart analysis.

- **The Library of Congress - History of Astrology:** (https://www.loc.gov) – Searchable records on the shift from "Mundane" (event) astrology to "Natal" (personality) astrology in the early 20th century.

Chapter 1

Printed Books

- **Arroyo, S. (1975).** *Astrology, Psychology, and the Four Elements.* CRCS Publications. (The definitive guide to elemental theory in modern astrology).

- **Greene, L. (1980).** *The Astrology of Fate.* (Explores the mythological roots of the elements and their relation to the Greek Fates).

- **Sasportas, H. (1985).** *The Twelve Houses.* (Contextualizes how the elements manifest specifically within different areas of life).

- **Hippocrates.** *The Humours.* (Various translations). (For those interested in the historical medical origins of temperament).

Scientific and Technical Resources

- **The Myers-Briggs Company:** (https://www.myersbriggs.org) – Research on psychological types (Sensation vs. Intuition, etc.) that directly correlate to the Earth/Fire/Air/Water archetypes.

- **The National Library of Medicine - History of Medicine:** (https://www.nlm.nih.gov) – Search for "The Four Humors" to see historical diagrams and medical texts on elemental balance.

- **The Kepler College of Astrological Arts and Sciences:** (https://www.keplercollege.org) – Provides academic papers on the mathematical calculation of elemental weighting in a birth chart.

Chapter 2

Printed Books

- **March, M., & McEvers, J. (1981).** The Only Way to Learn Astrology.

- **Tierney, B. (1983).** Dynamics of Aspect Analysis. (A technical look at how "T-Squares" between modalities create life-long character challenges).

- **Greene, L. (1984).** The Astrology of Fate. (Explores the mythological "Spinners" of fate and how they relate to the Cardinal, Fixed, and Mutable cycles of time).

Chapter 3

Printed Books

- **Spiller, J. (1997).** *Astrology for the Soul.* Bantam. (The most comprehensive guide to North Node placements ever written).

- **Arroyo, S. (1998).** *Astrology, Karma & Transformation.* (Explores the Nodes through a psychological and evolutionary lens).
- **Schulman, M. (1975).** *Karmic Astrology: The Moon's Nodes and Reincarnation.* Samuel Weiser. (A classic text for those interested in the deeper spiritual implications).

Chapter 4
Printed Books

- **Reinhart, M. (1989).** *Chiron and the Healing Journey.* Arkana. (The most in-depth psychological exploration of Chiron).
- **Hand, R. (1981).** *Essays on Astrology.* (Contains early technical data on Chiron's discovery and its astronomical classification).
- **Stein, Z. (1987).** *Essays on Chiron.* (Excellent for understanding Chiron's role in the "Return" at age 50).

Chapter 5
Printed Books

- **March, M., & McEvers, J. (1981).** *The Only Way to Learn Astrology, Vol 1.* ACS Publications. (Contains the most reliable manual calculation method for Signatures).
- **Hand, R. (1981).** *Horoscope Symbols.* Whitford Press. (A technical exploration of how "weighting" planets changes the interpretation of a chart).
- **Jung, C. G. (1921).** *Psychological Types.* (Essential for understanding the "Dominant Function" and how it mirrors the Signature Sign).

Online Sources

- **Astro-Seek Signature Sign Calculator:** https://horoscopes.astro-seek.com/signature-sign-astrology-calculator – A reliable digital tool for verifying your manual calculations.
- **The Faculty of Astrological Studies (UK):** https://www.astrology.org.uk – Offers academic articles on "Chart Synthesis" and the importance of identifying dominant energies.
- **Astro.com - "The Signature Sign":** https://www.astro.com/astrowiki/en/Signature_Sign – A comprehensive wiki entry on the history and various methods of calculating the Signature.

Conclusion

Printed Books

- **Arroyo, S. (1998).** *Astrology, Karma & Transformation.* CRCS Publications. (Provides the philosophical groundwork for integrating seemingly disparate chart factors).

- **Greene, L. (1993).** *The Inner Planets: Building Blocks of Personal Reality.* Seminar Series. (Deeply explores the internal "dialogue" between different parts of the psyche).

- **Hillman, J. (1996).** *The Soul's Code: In Search of Character and Calling.* Random House. (A vital text on why our "contradictions" and "wounds" are actually our destiny).

- **Hand, R. (1981).** *Horoscope Symbols.* Whitford Press. (A technical resource for understanding how to prioritize conflicting information in an astrological chart).

Online Sources

- **The Jung Center:** https://junghouston.org – Articles on "Individuation" and the process of reconciling internal opposites.

- **The Association for Psychological Astrology:** http://www.psychologicalastrology.com – Research papers on the correlation between astrological modalities and modern psychological archetypes.

- **Astro.com - "The Art of Synthesis":** https://www.astro.com/astrowiki/en/Synthesis – A technical breakdown of how to prioritize conflicting information in an astrological chart.

Reflection Questions

Printed Books

- **Mulligan, B. (1998).** *The Astrology of Midlife and Aging.* Llewellyn. (Great for reflecting on the Nodal and Chironic cycles).

- **Greene, L. (1977).** *Relating: An Astrological Guide to Living with Others on a Small Planet.* (Excellent questions on how our internal identity affects our relationships).

- **Arroyo, S. (1991).** *Chart Interpretation Handbook.* (A practical guide to synthesizing the scores you've calculated).

Reputable URL Sources

- **The Astrology Podcast - "Identifying Your Chart Signature":** https://theastrologypodcast.com – Search for episodes on chart synthesis for audio-based reflection.

- **The International Society for Astrological Research (ISAR):** https://isarastrology.org – Provides ethics and guidelines for deep self-reflective astrological work.

Workbook

Printed Books

- **Spiller, J. (1997).** *Astrology for the Soul.* (The definitive guide to the North and South Nodes).

- **Clow, B. H. (1987).** *Chiron: Rainbow Bridge Between the Inner & Outer Planets.* (Deep dive into the healing journey).

- **March, M., & McEvers, J. (1981).** *The Only Way to Learn Astrology, Vol 1.* (Great for manual scoring and tallying techniques).

Reputable URL Sources

- **Astro-Seek "Signature Sign Calculator":** https://horoscopes.astro-seek.com – For an automated check of your manual scores.

- **The Chiron Project:** https://www.chironandfriends.com – A community resource for understanding the "Wounded Healer" through various house placements.

Book 3

Introduction

Printed Books

- **Forrest, S. (1984).** *The Inner Sky.* Seven Paws Press. (A foundational text on choice-centered astrology and the dynamic nature of the chart).

- **Hand, R. (1976).** *Planets in Transit: Life Cycles for Living.* Whitford Press. (The comprehensive encyclopedia for understanding how planetary movements affect your natal placements).

- **Costello, D. (2012).** *Applied Astrology.* (Focuses on the practical, strategic application of astrology in career and personal decision-making).

- **Brady, B. (1999).** *Predictive Astrology: The Eagle and the Lark.* (An authoritative guide on the mechanics of transits and progressions).

Reputable URL Sources

- **The Mountain Astrologer - "Kairos and the Quality of Time":** https://mountainastrologer.com – Essays exploring the philosophical differences between chronological and astrological time.

- **Astrodienst - "Introduction to Transits":** https://www.astro.com/astrology/in_transits_e.htm – A technical overview of how current planetary positions interact with a natal chart.

- **The Astrology Podcast - "Timing Procedures":**
  https://theastrologypodcast.com – Search for episodes on "Annual
  Profections" and "Transits" for professional-level timing strategies.

Chapter 1

Printed Books

- **Greene, L. (1976).** *Saturn: A New Look at an Old Devil.* Samuel
  Weiser. (The absolute essential text for understanding the
  psychological "gift" of Saturn).

- **Sullivan, E. (1990).** *Saturn in Transit: Boundaries of Mind, Body, and
  Soul.* (A practical guide to how Saturn affects your specific house and
  sign placements).

- **Tierney, B. (1983).** *Dynamics of Aspect Analysis.* (Explores how
  Saturn's "squares" and "oppositions" create the tension necessary for
  growth).

Online Sources

- **Saturn Return Calculator:** https://www.astro-seek.com/saturn-return-
  astrology-calculator – Find the exact dates of your current or upcoming
  Saturn Return.

- **The Saturn Return Project:** https://www.saturnreturnproject.com – A
  community-based resource for sharing stories of the age-29 transition.

- **NASA Solar System Exploration - Saturn:**
  https://solarsystem.nasa.gov/planets/saturn/overview – For a deeper
  understanding of the physical properties of the "Lord of the Rings."

Chapter 2

Printed Books

- **Hand, R. (1976).** *Planets in Transit: Life Cycles for Living.* (The "Bible"
  of transits. Every student of astrology should own this).

- **Forrest, S. (2012).** *The Changing Sky.* (An excellent, storytelling-based
  approach to understanding planetary movement).

- **Lundsted, S. (1980).** *Transits: The Art of Forecasting.* (Focuses on the
  psychological impact of transits).

Reputable URL Sources

- **Astro-Seek Transit Chart Calculator:** https://horoscopes.astro-
  seek.com/transit-chart-astrology-calculator – The most accurate tool for
  seeing how today's planets "hit" your chart.

- **Cafe Astrology - Transits:** https://cafeastrology.com/transits.html – A
  beginner-friendly breakdown of what each transit means.

- **The Astrology Podcast - Transits Episode:**
  https://theastrologypodcast.com/2018/02/12/understanding-astrological-transits/ – A deep dive into the technical and philosophical nature of timing.

Chapter 3

Printed Books

- **Arroyo, S. (1984).** *Relationships and Life Cycles.* (Focuses on the psychological and energetic exchange between people).

- **Hand, R. (1975).** *Planets in Composite.* (The definitive guide to the "Third Entity" of a relationship).

- **Sakoian, F., & Acker, L. (1976).** *The Astrology of Human Relationships.* (A detailed technical manual for synastry aspects).

Reputable URL Sources

- **Astro-Seek Synastry Chart Calculator:** https://horoscopes.astro-seek.com/synastry-chart-online-calculator – An excellent tool for generating comparison charts.

- **The Faculty of Astrological Studies - Relationship Astrology:** https://www.astrology.org.uk – Search for articles on the ethics and depths of synastry.

- **Cafe Astrology - Synastry Symbols:** https://cafeastrology.com/synastry.html – A great beginner's guide to identifying key aspects between charts.

Chapter 4

Printed Books

- **Pottenger, M. (1994).** *Healing Mother-Father Issues through Astrology.* (Explores the relationship between the IC/MC axis and parental influence).

- **Arroyo, S. (1992).** *Exploring Astrology & Relationships.* (Contains excellent sections on how career and social standing impact our life path).

- **McEvers, J. (1989).** *Planets: The 10th House.* Llewellyn. (A deep technical dive into every possible placement in the house of career).

Reputable URL Sources

- **Astro-Seek Midheaven Calculator:** https://horoscopes.astro-seek.com/midheaven-sign-calculator – Find your MC sign and degree instantly.

- **The Astrology Podcast - The 10th House:** https://theastrologypodcast.com – Search for the episode on the 10th house and MC for a professional-level discussion on vocational astrology.

- **Astro.com - "The Midheaven":** https://www.astro.com/astrowiki/en/Midheaven – A comprehensive wiki entry on the astronomy and history of the MC.

Chapter 5
Printed Books

- **Hastings, N. J. (1984).** *The Secondary Progressed Chart.* (A clear, technical manual for calculating and interpreting progressions).

- **Brady, B. (1999).** *Predictive Astrology: The Eagle and the Lark.* (Excellent sections on the "Progressed Lunation Cycle").

- **Forrest, S. (2018).** *The Book of the Moon.* (Deeply explores the 27-year cycle of the Progressed Moon).

Reputable URL Sources

- **Astro-Seek Secondary Progressions Calculator:** https://horoscopes.astro-seek.com/secondary-progressions-astrology-calculator – Generate your current progressed chart.

- **Astrodienst - "The Progressed Moon through the Houses":** https://www.astro.com – Search their library for Dana Gerhardt's excellent series on the Progressed Moon.

- **The Astrology Podcast - Secondary Progressions:** https://theastrologypodcast.com – Episode #198 provides a comprehensive historical and practical overview.

Conclusion
Printed Books

- **Pallis, M. (1995).** *Celestial Charts: Antique Maps of the Heavens.* (For visual inspiration on the history of cosmic navigation).

- **Tarnas, R. (2006).** *Cosmos and Psyche: Intimations of a New World View.* (The definitive philosophical work on the correlation between planetary cycles and human history).

- **Forrest, S. (2020).** *The Captain and the Sky.* (Explores the role of free will and personal agency within the framework of astrological timing).

URL Sources

- **The International Society for Astrological Research (ISAR):** https://isarastrology.org – Resources for the continued ethical study of astrology.

- **NASA/JPL Horizons System:** https://ssd.jpl.nasa.gov/horizons/ – For highly precise ephemeral data on planetary positions for the next century.
- **The Organization for Professional Astrology (OPA):** https://opaastrology.org – Articles on integrating astrology into professional life and vocational planning.

Reflection

Printed Books

- **Lineman, R. (1984).** *Evolutionary Astrology.* (Focuses on the long-term spiritual purpose of the life cycles we've discussed).
- **Mulligan, B. (1998).** *The Astrology of Midlife and Aging.* (Essential for reflecting on the larger planetary cycles of adulthood).
- **Sasportas, H. (1985).** *The Twelve Houses.* (Provides the reflective depth needed to understand where your transits are landing).

URL Sources

- **The Jung Center:** https://junghouston.org – Resources for deep psychological self-reflection and archetypal study.
- **The Association for Psychological Astrology:** http://www.psychologicalastrology.com – Scholarly articles on integrating chart data with personal growth.
- **Astro-Seek "Personal Transit Calendar":** https://horoscopes.astro-seek.com – A tool to map your specific timing for the next 12 months.

Workbook

Printed Books

- **Hand, R. (1981).** *Horoscope Symbols.* (An essential reference for the planetary glyphs used in this workbook).
- **Forrest, S. (2012).** *The Changing Sky.* (Helpful for interpreting the "Personal Goals" sections of the calendar).
- **Greene, L. (2003).** *The Astrology of Fate.* (On the philosophy of using a "Purpose Planner" to navigate life's inevitable turns).

Reputable URL Sources

- **Astro-Seek "Free Astrology Calendar":** https://horoscopes.astro-seek.com – To find the specific dates for Part 1.
- **The Astrology Podcast - "How to Read a Transit Calendar":** https://theastrologypodcast.com – A visual/audio guide for beginners.
- **NASA's JPL Horizons:** https://ssd.jpl.nasa.gov – For the scientific precision of planetary orbits.

Overall Conclusion

Printed Books

- **Tarnas, R. (2006).** *Cosmos and Psyche.* Viking Press. (The most important modern philosophical defense of astrology's role in human history).

- **Hillman, J. (1996).** *The Soul's Code.* Random House. (A masterpiece on the "acorn theory" of personality—the idea that our destiny is encoded within us).

- **Eisler, R. (1987).** *The Chalice and the Blade.* (For historical context on how we moved from cyclical, nature-based time to linear time).

Reputable URL Sources

- **The Sophia Centre for the Study of Cosmology in Culture:** https://www.uwtsd.ac.uk/sophia/ – For those interested in the academic and historical study of astrology.

- **The Faculty of Astrological Studies:** https://www.astrology.org.uk – A world-renowned institution for continuing your technical education.

- **OPAL (Organization for Professional Astrology):** https://opaastrology.org – For community support and ethical guidelines as you share your knowledge with others.